A Fearful Symmetry,

The Complementarity of Men and Women in Ministry

A. M. ALLCHIN   SANDRA FIGGISS
KALLISTOS WARE   WENDY ROBINSON
GEOFFREY ROWELL   STEPHEN VERNEY
ROSEMARY WICKREMASINGHE   LINDA WOODHEAD
GRAHAM WOOLFENDEN

Foreword by
JOHN V. TAYLOR

First published in Great Britain 1992
Society for Promoting Christian Knowledge
Holy Trinity Church
Marylebone Road
London NW1 4DU

British Library Cataloguing-in-Publication Data

A catalogue record for this book is available
from the British Library

ISBN 0-281-04651-4

Typeset by Pioneer Associates, Perthshire
Printed in Great Britain by
Hart-Talbot Ltd, Saffron Walden, Essex

Contents

Members of the group
who have signed this Report:

Dr A M Allchin

Director of the St Theosevia Centre for Christian Spirituality, Oxford; Honorary Canon of Canterbury Cathedral; Honorary Professor of the University College of North Wales, Bangor.

Sister Sandra Figgess

Member of the Society of the Sacred Heart, Oxford; founder member of Arc Ecumenical Community; welfare rights worker.

Bishop Kallistos of Diokleia

Assistant Bishop in the Orthodox Archdiocese of Thyateira and Great Britain; Fellow of Pembroke College, Oxford; Spalding Lecturer in Eastern Orthodox Studies at the University of Oxford.

Wendy Robinson

Psychotherapist and Pastoral Counsellor; Lecturer in Pastoral Studies at Ripon College, Cuddesdon; member of the congregation of the Orthodox Church in Oxford.

Canon Dr Geoffrey Rowell

Chaplain and Fellow, Keble College, Oxford; University Lecturer in Theology; member of the Church of England Liturgical Commission 1980 – 90; member of the Church of England Doctrine Commission from 1990.

Bishop Stephen Verney

Formerly Bishop of Repton; author; founder-member of The Abbey, Sutton Courtenay.

Rosemary Wickremasinghe

Member of the community at The Abbey, Sutton Courtenay; painter concerned with theology and the spiritual life.

Linda Woodhead

Lecturer in Christian Studies at the Department of Religious Studies in the University of Lancaster; formerly Lecturer in Christian Doctrine and Ethics at Ripon College, Cuddesdon.

The Reverend Graham Woolfenden

Roman Catholic priest; Lecturer in Liturgy and Worship at the Anglican theological college, Ripon College, Cuddesdon.

Foreword

by Bishop John V Taylor

This Report is not, thank God, a last-minute ploy to sway the General Synod's vote for or against the ordination of women to the priesthood. It breathes an entirely different atmosphere from that of the hustings. It is in fact a model of what should have been taking place in every diocese and all the major cities in place of the campaign approach to decision-making.

Here are five women and five men, well-qualified for the task, drawn from the Roman Catholic, Orthodox, Anglican and United Reformed communions in Oxfordshire, who have been meeting regularly for the past three years and now share their insights. Instead of deploying arrogantly rigid certainties, they re-opened the questions to uncover the underlying issues — the nature of the mutuality of men and women and the meaning of ministerial priesthood. Instead of winning arguments they have come to recognize and value God's truth in each other. They have not resolved their differences but transcended them through their delight in the unity of spirit which they have discovered.

For two reasons this small book should be required reading, in the Church of England at least. First, because it may bring us as a Church to profound repentance for the wantonly adversarial style in which we have chosen to handle every issue of church order since the Anglican-Methodist scheme of 1967 – 8. Second, because this study group, which included a woman ordained to the Free Church ministry, has demonstrated that, whichever decision our synod takes in November, Christians can, and must, stay together in ecumenical discussion of this temper.

Tyger! Tyger! burning bright
In the forests of the night,
What immortal hand or eye,
Dare frame thy fearful symmetry?
WILLIAM BLAKE

Introduction

The ordination of women to the priesthood has become an acute and painful problem within the Anglican Church. The difficulty at the heart of the debate is that we do not really understand what we are talking about.

In 1988 Donald Allchin and Stephen Verney, both lovers of Anglican spirituality in its 'height and depth, length and breadth', approached Wendy Robinson (an Orthodox) and decided with her to set up an inter-Church group to explore this question.

We would meet on the basis that within the words 'the ordination of women to the priesthood' there lie hidden two mysteries. The first is the mystery of masculine/feminine. The more we discuss these concepts and try to define them, the more we say 'Not that, not that'. Over the last decade we have come to accept that what are conventionally labelled masculine and feminine are found together in each man and each woman. But beyond that, and deeper, what is the difference between holding this balance in a male body or holding it in a female one? In the end, as in the beginning, what does it mean that 'God created the human person in his own image, male and female created He them' (Genesis 1.27)?

The second mystery is that of priesthood. Many Christians do not feel at home with that word, and prefer to talk of ministry. But others, including Orthodox, Roman Catholics and Anglicans, sense that in the concept of priesthood lies hidden some deep truth about the intercourse between God and humankind.

The word 'mystery' is to be used in its proper sense – as a secret too deep to be grasped by the human intellect, but out of which God reveals to us the truth about Himself. So, quite literally, in this debate we are not able to 'understand' what we are talking about.

We felt that the group should be not more than ten, so that we might be able to get to know and trust one another and enter into a real conversation. We should be male and female, drawn from different Christian stand-points. We would invite Anglicans who were known to start from opposite sides in the 'ordination of women' debate. We would invite a number of Roman Catholics and Orthodox to come and help us, knowing that they too are concerned about these issues, and because we were also conscious of the deep conviction of many Anglicans that any decision in this area should be taken jointly by the Roman Catholic, Orthodox and Anglican Churches together. Could we at least make a start by inviting members of these three Churches to meet unofficially as persons, and with the aim of sharing our faith and our experience, and exposing ourselves and our uncertainties to these two mysteries of God?

We would confront together the question of the ordination of women to the priesthood but, learning from our past experience, we would not charge at it like the proverbial bull at the gate. In order to approach the problem within a wider and deeper framework, we chose as the title for our discussions 'The Complementarity of Men and Women in Ministry: What Sort of Ministry Does God Want?'

We decided to invite people from Oxfordshire (where we all live), and in answer to the first round of invitations the local Orthodox and Roman Catholic Bishops both agreed to join us. Shortly after, the Roman Catholic Bishop was translated to another diocese, but we were able to act on his advice in inviting our Roman Catholic colleagues. The group finally crystallized as five men and five women. They were drawn from the three Churches already mentioned, and also included a woman Free Church minister who was able to be with us for most of our discussions, but not the final stages when the report was drafted. Perhaps crystal, with its sparkle and its many facets, is not a bad image of our meetings over the next three years.

In what follows, it is not to be assumed that every member of our group is in full agreement with each sentence. But all of us feel able to endorse this joint report as a true record of the direction taken by our discussions. Although we may not always have achieved a 'common mind', we did indeed come to a renewed sense of a unity within and beyond all differences.

PART ONE
Unity in Diversity

The group, and how it worked

We have met twelve times over three years. Our usual pattern was to assemble on a Friday afternoon about four o'clock, and to engage in an intellectual and theological debate until supper. After supper we would meet in a more relaxed manner, round an open fire in winter-time, sharing music, poems, icons and symbols which had been significant for each of us, or exploring our own experience – and, indeed, ourselves – as far as each one might wish to do so. We would end the day with some form of evening prayer. The next morning began with a period of silent mediation and continued after breakfast with a second theological debate, introduced by a paper from one of our members. After the coffee break we discussed 'Where do we go from here?' 'What are the questions emerging which must be addressed next time?' 'When can ten impossibly busy people find time to meet?' It was significant that we *wanted* to meet, because the questions were so deeply important to us, and the company so good and so rich in its variety and openness.

The membership was not absolutely consistent but it has regularly comprised five men and five women divided denominationally as follows: two Orthodox, two or three Roman Catholics, one United Reformed and four or five Anglicans.

Our discussion has taken place in the context of the controversy over the possible ordination of women to the priesthood and episcopate in the Church of England. The controversy is one which is felt as deeply painful on both sides, and the decisions which must be made – whichever way they go – will inevitably cause pain. But our discussion has convinced us that the pain of our present disagreement need not be a blind pain. This particular question is part of a larger series of questions about the relationship between men and women in the Church and society. Many things are changing, and some at least of these changes we believe to be good and some of the pain is the pain of new growth. Through patient work and careful discrimination can come new life which blossoms and bears fruit.

Our group itself was a sign, however small, of a situation which is changing. Thirty-five years ago an English Orthodox bishop, a laywoman teaching theology in an Anglican theological college, a Roman Catholic woman religious with experience of preaching, a woman minister of the United Reformed

3

Church, could not have sat down and discussed these things together. As a matter of fact, nobody was then filling any of these roles: the United Reformed Church did not yet exist, there was no Englishman who was an Orthodox bishop, Roman Catholic women did not have the experience of preaching and, although they sometimes taught ancillary subjects in Anglican theological colleges, women did not normally teach the basic theological disciplines.

Moreover, it was not only the fact of our meeting which was new. The form which our meetings took was also new. We found that it was not only *valuable* but also *necessary* to approach the subject in a variety of ways:

(a) We followed the classical path of Christian controversy, looking at our interpretation of the Scripture, our understanding of tradition, and our use of arguments from reason and experience.
(b) We also shared more personally our own experience of life as men and women, married and unmarried.
(c) We prayed and meditated together.
(d) We approached questions imaginatively through our appreciation of the arts and of symbols both poetic and visual. As one of us wrote:

It was illuminating to use a logical approach, but we recognized also that this subject touches our hearts and wills and our imagination. One of the strengths of the group has been that we have used many different modes of discourse, both rational and symbolic, visual and aural, as well as verbal methods. Only such a wide mix can hope to capture the immense complexities, paradoxes and antinomies that are held between men and woman. As we are made in God's image, and bear that image between us, it is only to be expected that formulations which are intellectually satisfying are never going to express the necessary apophatic hesitation before the depths of the mystery.

These more personal approaches added a new dimension to our meetings, contributing to our sense that the consideration of this controverted question can be more fruitful than we had expected. As one member commented:

We have been engaged in two ways of talking, the experiential and the way of logical analysis. They interact as the married and the single interact; as the two different ways of thinking and feeling about God, Logos and Sophia, interact. Is Christianity a meeting of many things, not only of what we say but of different ways of saying it?

It was fruitful not because we solved the controversy in the sense of coming to a unanimous answer, but because, within the controversy itself and our inability to solve it, we experienced the truth of God holding us together. This does not imply a facile compromise. In spite of the possibility of mutual incomprehension, different people gave weight to different insights. One of us wrote:

> My own position has not moved during the sessions. What I think I have learned is something about the nature of the controversy: that we are all making perfectly logical, reasonable, valid moves on a chess-board, but that we are all playing on different chess-boards and therefore our arguments do not really touch one another. Or, putting it another way, we do not share the same starting point or the same basic premises and we are not actually asking the same questions . . . .
>
> We have talked often about 'Scripture and tradition' as competing or complementary authorities; but it seems to me that our discussions highlight that for us the competing authorities are the past and the present. For some of us the central question is 'How is God present in the world today? How is God calling us now?' The past is valued to the extent that it illuminates the present, but the past cannot be allowed to impede the movement of the Spirit in the now-time. For others of us it is the past that is authoritative – and the responsibility of the present generation is to pass on the past to the future without compromising its integrity.
>
> I think that it is this fundamental difference in approach, even more than our varying positions along the spectrum of whether the differences between men and women are more or less significant than the similarities, which underlies our positions on the role of women in ministry, and on the nature of priestly ministry in our day.

Others of us were unwilling to contrast past and present in this way. The past and the present are both alike authoritative, and our God 'who was, and who is, and who is to come' (Revelation 4.8) holds them together in Himself. Another of us wrote:

> This group experience has kindled hope in me that people of widely divergent views can stay together and explore with mutual benefit some of the complex problems and mysteries of man, woman, priesthood. The mysteries remain too deep to provide simple answers. We need time and patience with each other even to begin to unravel some of the threads before we weave new patterns. . . .
>
> Theology has to face new questions. After research the tradition proves to be silent. There is no escape from the fact that we all find ourselves under the hand of God, trying to discern the movement of the Spirit. That should undercut our more arrogant certainties. I need experiences like the one provided by this group to give me hope that such a waiting on God might be possible even in our hasty contemporary world.

Unity in Diversity

A new question

We recognized that the subject was in nearly every way a new one, and has arisen only within this century. In England it was in 1917 that the first woman was ordained in the Congregationalist Church; in the Presbyterian Church the same such ordination took place in 1961. In the Church of England the first official discussion of the question took place in 1920. It was only in the 1960s that the discussion became general. For the greater part of Christian history there has been no question to discuss. During the first centuries of the Church's life and in the emergence of the threefold ministry of Bishop, Priest and Deacon, there seems never to have been a formal decision about this subject, though the question is occasionally raised. The ordained ministry in all the Churches has belonged to men. The Churches of the Reformation which rejected the threefold ministry did not question this part of the tradition — and, indeed, the ministry of women became more restricted. The Quakers were one of the very few groups who raised the matter before the twentieth century.

The silence of the tradition struck us all as very significant. But significant of what? Had there been no question to discuss for two thousand years because it was culturally impossible to discuss it, and because the social position of women made it inconceivable that they could exercise such leadership roles in the Church? Did the silence of the tradition leave us free to raise this as a new question in our generation? Or should we draw the opposite conclusion: that the living tradition is not just a set of man-made rules but springs out of the profound and eternal truth about men and women and priesthood in the mind of God? Have we the right to innovate so radically? Though we all agree that the Holy Spirit acts through the world, and therefore through modern sociological insights, should we not also recognize the presence of Satan and his angels as active in our world, and the growth of the demonic in our society? The world (the *kosmos* in the Johannine sense) should not guide our agenda.

Yet the role of women within the tradition and within Church history has not been passive. In the earlier centuries, particularly in the East, the ordination of women as deaconesses gave them a certain standing in the life of the Church. In the West, in both early and more recent centuries, there have been women who as abbesses or founders of religious orders have played a significant part in the public life of the Church. However, the suggestion that women could and should be integrated into the historic order of Bishop, Priest and Deacon has simply not been made.

We are living in a new time, since in all our Churches this suggestion is being made. In all our Churches, at least in some respects, the position of women is changing, and laywomen and women in religious orders are coming to adopt new roles in the public life of the Church.

The most obvious example of this is in theological teaching, since in all the Churches there is an increasing number of women who are highly trained theologians. It is a remarkable fact that, in many of our university theological courses, there is now a preponderance of women over men students. This again would have been unthinkable fifty years ago, and it expresses a profound change happening in the Orthodox East as well as in the Catholic and Protestant West: that women at all social and intellectual levels are claiming theology as their concern no less than that of men. Recently one of us who has known Greece for fifty years revisited friends, a peasant family from a mountain village; as in the past, the women-folk cooked the meal while the men drank and talked politics. But then something new happened: after supper the women joined the men at the table, and the daughter of the house told their guest that she was planning to study theology.

The changed position of women within the Churches reflects their changed position in the world at large. In all our societies it is accepted that women can and should fulfil roles in public life, in government and the professions, in the judiciary, in business and commerce, in the field of publicity and the arts, which a century ago would have been the preserve men. Indeed, while the group was discussing the final draft of this report, the first Madam Speaker was elected. These changes are parallel to changes in personal life and experience and understanding. Areas of human experience are finding articulation in ways which are altogether new. Even a woman's experience of giving birth is expressed in new ways.

Complementarity

So, in the Churches at large, men and women enter into new and more equal relationships of reciprocity and interdependence. Our own meetings have been a small part of the process. We have not in general found that our recognition of personal equality has involved any diminution of our recognition of personal difference and diversity. We have found our complementarity within the group enriching and rewarding. We believe that the recognition of mutuality in difference between men and women in the Church is part of a wider movement of recognition of our need for one another across our differences – as between married and single, for instance, or as between people of different races and cultures.

The word *complementarity* itself is not without its problems. One of our number has noted:

Complementarity between men and women has unfortunately often been used as a euphemism for dominance and subjugation — as though complementarity is best exemplified by the men leading the congregation and the women making the tea . . . or teaching the children. Complementarity then becomes a matter of role or function so that certain ministries are thought to be proper to men, while other complementary ministries are thought to be proper to women. . . . But should we not rather look for complementarity of approach and style within any particular role or function? The Church needs to hear both men and women breaking open the word in the homily or sermon. All preachers will have their own distinctive style, which enriches the total experience of hearing the word of God. There is certainly no one particular style which is common to all women preachers – but where women are regularly included in this aspect of ministry, the range of issues addressed, the experiential base from which the word is proclaimed, and the variety of approaches and styles are greatly extended.

The Churches thus live in societies in which the role of women is rapidly changing. These changes do not of themselves dictate what changes, if any, the Churches should make in the ordering of their own inner life. Indeed, they may suggest that the Churches should remain true to the dynamic of their own inner nature, which is different from that of society at large. They do, however, provide a new context in which the Churches' life is set, and affect the significance of the decisions which the Churches make. For the Church to have an all-male ministry, in a society where in general all offices are open to women as well as men, may be the will of God for his Church, but it will certainly differentiate the Church from society in a way it has not been differentiated before.

The coincidence of opposites

We return to the title of our discussions, 'The Complementarity of Men and Women in Ministry'. What is the mysterious complementarity between men and women? The more we explored it, the more we found ourselves polarizing towards opposites. Some of us tended to the belief that men and women are essentially similar, as human beings sharing the same complex human nature. Others of us were of the belief that they are ontologically different, guardians in their embodiment of certain distinctive realities, and that erotic attraction between men and women is a sign of this profound difference, with all the colour and richness it brings to human life.

Once again we must ask: What might our God have to say about these opposites? — our God who 'created the human person in His own image, male and female He created them', and of whom it is said: 'All things go in pairs, one the counterpart of the other, and He has made nothing incomplete; each confirms the virtues of the other' (Ecclesiasticus 42.24 – 5). Nicolas of Cusa writing about 1440, sees God as the *coincidentia oppositorum*, the coincidence of opposites; in God, all distinctions are contained and transcended in an ultimate truth, in the world we are unfolding in diversity what is enfolded in the oneness of God. Five hundred years later Niels Böhr, speaking as a quantum physicist in our own time, insists: 'The opposite of a correct statement is a false statement, but the opposite of a profound truth may well be another profound truth.'

The mediaeval theologian and the quantum physicist both believe that there is a mysterious complementarity which underlies the reality of the universe, but which cannot be grasped by the human mind. Nicolas expounds on the incomprehensibility of God in his work 'on learned ignorance', *De Docta Ignorantia*. We know about what God is not rather than what he is. We can say affirmatively that God is the *coincidentia oppositorum*, but we cannot measure how these opposites are proportioned in God or apply to Him. Niels Böhr sees in physics the 'Principle of Complementarity': that the nature of matter is both wave-like and particle-like; that these two ways of describing it complement each other; and that the whole picture emerges only when one way provides the information which the other lacks. But at the same time he expounds the 'Uncertainty Principle': that the exact properties of matter cannot be measured. For, although we need two complementary ways of looking at matter to get the whole picture, only one way is available at a time. If you know how fast a particle is moving, you cannot know where it is; while if you know where it is then you cannot know how fast it is moving.

Both of them, as they try to look at the reality of how things are, see a basic complementarity, but they tell us that this complementarity is itself incomprehensible. Nicolas describes the coincidence of opposites, which reason and logic abhor, as the 'wall' beyond which the soul finds God, coming by reason and experience to know the unknowable and to realize the necessity of the impossible. The quantum physicist warns us that the very act of observation collapses the complementarity that we are looking at. As we try to observe quantum systems in their wave and particle duality, our consciousness collapses the wave-like function with all its possibilities, and changes those systems into ordinary and limited objects.

Does this suggest anything to those of us looking at men, women and priesthood? When we find ourselves advocating truths which appear to be opposites, may they nevertheless coincide in God? May God's truth in its wholeness be able to emerge only because we are looking at it in different ways? By our different ways of looking, may we not only be providing for each other the information which the other lacks, but actually be co-operating with God as, out of the riches of His glory, He evokes into being different possibilities and complementary realities?

As we follow the thought of Nicolas of Cusa, the word 'complementarity' becomes for us a description of God, a name under which the mystery of His Being lies hidden. No wonder, then, that complementarity eludes our comprehension, and that when we try to analyse and define it the living reality collapses. The quantum physicists tell us that complementarity is changed as we observe it, but Nicolas tells us that *we* are changed as Complementarity observes us. In his treatise entitled *The Gaze of God, De Visione Dei*, he understands the 'vision' not primarily as our vision of God but as God's vision of us. His subtitle is *The Icon* and he likens God's presence to the eye in a picture or icon which seems to follow the observers as they move, and to 'see' all simultaneously without moving.

Nicolas had arrived at his profound theology through the marriage of his own experience 'from on high' with the writings of the Rhineland mystics, and those of St Dionysius the Areopagite. He represents an approximation in the West to the apophatic tradition of Eastern Orthodoxy expressed by St Maximus the Confessor and St Gregory Palamas. This made him eager for the unity and the reform of the Church. He has been described recently by a Jesuit scholar as 'five hundred years ahead of ecumenical thought'. With a similar concern for the coincidence of opposites, Palamas said of God: 'He is both existent and non-existent; He is everywhere and nowhere; He has many names and He cannot be named; He is ever-moving and He is immovable; and in a word He is everything and nothing.'

As we, five hundred years later, have been struggling to reconcile our differences, meeting under the title 'The Complementarity of Men and Women in Ministry', Nicolas seems to be suggesting that both parties may be right and both wrong, but that in any case struggling will not enable us to answer the question in our sub-title, 'What sort of a ministry does God want?' Complementarity is looking at us. Reconciling opposites is God's work, not ours.

So in Part Two, as we focus on six themes which have emerged in our discussion and which we think are the context in which 'right' decisions must be made, we will try to sort out the opposites – not to reconcile them.

/

PART TWO
Diversity in Unity

1
Men and women

One member of our group wrote:

> It seems to me that there is a crucial issue which has to be addressed before
> any judgement can be made about the appropriate ministries for men and
> women: are there any significant differences between the sexes and, if so,
> what are they? If men and women really are different – not only physically
> but also psychologically and spiritually – then it would be reasonable to
> expect that women will have very different ministries from men.
>
> If, however, it is impossible to show that there are any fixed differences
> between the sexes apart from the obvious physical ones, then it is
> inappropriate to speak of 'women's ministry' as if it were a different sort of
> thing from men's ministry'. Different individuals will have different
> ministries, but they cannot be specified in advance simply on the basis of
> gender. No woman should therefore be excluded from the ordained ministry
> simply because she is a woman; like a man she should be judged by the
> Church on her suitability for this special ministry.

Our first theme is men and women. From what starting point can we begin?
For, as we have already suggested, the starting point will affect the conclusion.
So let us begin from the words 'In the beginning':

> In the beginning God created the human person in His own image: in the
> image of God He created him; male and female He created them.
>
> (Genesis 1.27).

In these words we are confronted by the two problems which underlie our
whole debate. First, that God is referred to in male language – we will return
to this later. Second, that both sides of our 'crucial issue' seem to be affirmed.
God creates human nature to reflect His own nature ('in His own image'). He

11

who is the coincidence of opposites creates human beings who are essentially similar to each other, who all experience heat and cold, fear and love, and yet who are ontologically different. 'Male and female created He them.' Both this similarity and this difference arise out of the nature of God, and are called into being by God's own fiat.

This text is quoted by Jesus as the fundamental truth about men and women (Matthew 19.4; Mark 10.6). They are complementary and, through their relationship together, reveal God's image. They will reveal that image of love through the to-and-fro by which they will become one, 'Therefore a man shall leave his father and mother and be joined to his wife, and they shall become one flesh' (Matthew 19.5). This love is both *eros*, erotic love through which they will procreate, and *agape*, the love through which they see God in each other and by which they set free in each other God's loving presence. This complementarity of male and female may be expressed both through marriage and also through celibacy. Celibacy should be seen as quite different from unisex and adrogyny, for in these concepts the interplay of masculine and feminine (that may be found even in a single person's wholeness) is obscured and so, therefore, is the image of God's glory that may be found in that single person.

The changing position of women in society

Over the course of this century, particularly in the developed countries, the position of women in society has been changing. Gradually it has become possible for women to adopt roles and take up social positions formerly reserved for men, particularly those of power and authority. Women have become much freer to choose the sort of life they wish to lead and to break away from the controlling influence of men.

Without any doubt this change in women's status is one of the biggest changes ever to affect human society. It has had a direct effect not only on many of the structures of that society but on the lives of every man and woman within it. Given the magnitude of the change, it is perhaps surprising that, once under way, it has occasioned relatively little public debate and overt resistance in the secular world.

Perhaps the reason is that the emancipation of women has been seen primarily as a clear matter of social justice. As such, the issue has appeared quite simple: men and women have equal rights, but throughout the course of human history these rights have been systematically denied to women; this injustice must now be righted. Anyone who disagrees with this presentation of the matter is in danger of being branded an opponent of justice.

In the Church things have been very different. The change in women's status – especially within the Church – has been fiercely opposed by many, and the appeal to social justice in the secular world has often been rejected. The position of women within the Church has changed far more slowly than it has outside the Church. As a consequence, the Church now stands isolated within society. Some see this as a brave witness; others as suicidal conservatism.

It may, however, be possible for people on both sides of the debate to agree that the Church's cautious reaction to the change in women's status has been a wise one in at least two ways.

First, it has been right not to regard the appeal to social justice as final. Social justice and equal rights are post-Enlightenment notions and, though they may have roots within the Christian tradition, they are not ethical notions that can be directly drawn from that tradition. It is entirely appropriate, therefore, that the Church should evaluate the appropriateness of women's changing roles in society, using its own categories of ethical evaluation (such as complementarity) and its own understanding of truth.

Second, the serious debate within the Church concerning women's roles has been appropriate to the magnitude of the changes proposed – in a way that the silent acquiescence to change on the part of wider society has perhaps not. The debate has acknowledged that the ordination of women is not simply a minor question about Church order, but has much wider implications and repercussions for the Christian faith and the living out of the faith. It touches the lives of Christian men and women at every level. The writer of the Epistle to the Hebrews has already alerted us to the consequences: 'The priesthood being changed, there is also a change of the law' (Hebrews 7.12).

Are there differences between the sexes?

It is surprising how little systematic critical reflection has until recently been given to the question of the difference – or lack of difference – between the sexes. This is true both within and outside the Church. Yet this question is of quite fundamental importance to any discussion of the appropriateness of changing women's roles in Church and society, for if there is little significant difference between men and women then there is clearly no reason why they should be allotted different roles. However, if there *are* differences, it will be important to specify what they are, so that it can be seen which roles are appropriate for men and which for women.

Often people assume that there are important differences between the sexes. This is portrayed by comments such as 'I like women to be women' or 'he's a real man'. The fact that pair-bonding between a man and a woman is a constant feature of human societies, and is also found in the animal kingdom, adds weight to this belief that there is a natural complementarity based on difference between the sexes. Several of us felt intuitively that the genders are different, and were content to describe this difference as a mysterious one. Both men and women agreed on how different it feels to be exclusively with members of one's own sex: the conversation is different, the interests are different, the dynamics are different. But the task of spelling out exactly what the differences are proved controversial. We explored at least four different avenues.

Biological and bodily differences

The most obvious differences between men and women are biological. Men and women have different primary and secondary sexual characteristics.

Some would want to go further than this, and argue that there are psychological differences between the sexes, flowing from the physical differences, which might carry spiritual significance. For example, putting the matter in a simplified form, it might be claimed:

(a) Because in sexual intercourse men 'give' and women 'receive', men are more generally disposed to be more active and initiative-taking, whilst women are disposed to be passive and receptive.

(b) The fact that women can bear and give birth to children fosters in them qualities such as patience, greater harmony with the body and with nature, nurturing tendencies, and so on.

(c) The pains of childbirth and menstruation are reasons why women are more long-suffering and aware of their finitude than men.

Others of us were suspicious of arguments like these which generalize from biological differences to psychological ones. People's characters seem to be formed by their culture, upbringing and free choice as well as by their bodily functions. Moreover, these bodily functions may themselves be deeply influenced by culture: for example, it is only in a particular masculine culture that a man would interpret intercourse as giving something to a passive recipient.

Similarly, the upbringing of children may not be a 'natural' or 'biological' role for women but one imposed by culture. Recent changes in patterns of child-rearing would support this. Nature and culture appear to be interwoven in a complementarity and a complexity which cannot be unravelled, but which demand deep and prayerful attention as we reflect that between us as men and women we carry the image of God, so that differences as well as likenesses must be significant.

Whatever our assessment of the psychological implications of bodily differences, we were all of us anxious, as Christians, to avoid a dualist anthropology which sees the body as something separate from (and inferior to) the soul. We preferred to think of men and women as necessarily embodied beings. If this is so, the bodily differences between men and women imply that men and women *are* different; it is not possible to dismiss the differences as 'merely bodily'.

Cognitive differences

It is often said that men and women arrive at knowledge by different routes. The most common belief seems to be that women work by intuition and feeling, men by reason and logic.

Some of the women in the group were resistant to this suggestion, believing themselves to be as rational as any man. They felt that it might have been possible to believe that women were less rational in the days when they were denied proper education, but we now know that women can compete with men on equal terms in intellectual endeavour.

Others of us – both men and women – believed that women were more in touch with their feelings than men. Women seemed more able to express these feelings without shame, and to take them into account when making judgements. But this may be dictated by our culture. In books about the Jewish Kabbalah a diagram of the human body is often shown in which the masculine characteristics are listed down one side and the feminine down the other, and surprisingly intuition appears on the masculine side and reason on the feminine. This suggests, contrary to our usual assumptions, that the male character or cultural role more naturally allows for flashes of intuition, while the female character or cultural role has the more stable functions of containing and ordering.

Different priorities in life

Another possibility we explored is that men and women differ in their priorities, and in the value they ascribe to different things. We could perhaps detect this in the different topics of conversation chosen by all-male and all-female groups: whilst the former tend to talk about jobs and the external happenings of life, the latter tend to talk about relationships.

We noticed that men give a high priority to their careers, to which they are likely to devote a great deal of time, commitment and energy. They often get caught up in the politics of the workplace; they are likely to see failure in their careers as deeply demeaning. In all these ways, men seem to gain their sense of self-worth from their personal achievement in the public world. This achievement may be thought of in material terms – having a nice house, a big car, money in the bank – or in other ways such as making a contribution to scholarship, being honoured, or just doing a good job.

Women, on the other hand, seem not to set so much store by their jobs or careers. They are often reluctant to work excessive hours (which is one of the reasons for the lack of women in the Stock Exchange or Parliament). They are more likely to be dismissive of politics at work; they do not find failure in this sphere as undermining as do men. So, in contrast to a large number of men, women appear to get their sense of self-worth from relationships, particularly intimate relationships. When they do choose to pursue a career, it is likely to be a caring one or one that is to do with people. They often see the value of their work in terms of the relationships it enables them to form; they are more likely than men to give up their jobs to look after a husband, child or relative, and more likely to pity someone who hasn't had children, or who hasn't found a partner, than someone who has failed in their career.

In these different tendencies of men and women we can notice on both sides the pluses and minuses. Women, because they dwell more on relationships, may find it harder to forget an insult, and easier to become unhealthily dependent or to create dependencies. Men can be so concerned with work that they neglect others and take no account of their feelings: women who have worked in all-male environments have noted this.

Different self-estimation

Some of the women in our group noted that women often seem to have a far lower view of themselves and their abilities than do men. In teaching other women, they had noticed how lacking they were in self-confidence; they are often reluctant to express themselves, particularly verbally, and need a great deal of encouragement and affirmation. In discussion groups it is generally the men who speak and the women who listen. It has also been observed that women speak at less length and are interrupted more because they use more hesitant speech patterns, which allow for doubt and the desire for dialogue, but which also seem to betray a self-doubt which proves unconvincing to the methods of such male discourse. Others of us who had been spiritual counsellors to women had noticed this same lack of self-confidence. However, it was remarked that women are much more likely to laugh at themselves (and at men) and to puncture pomposity.

The deepest theological issue at stake here is that of *kenosis*, self-emptying, dying to self, which is central to our Christology. For men, that doctrine often involves a wrestle with power and its expression in dialogue. For women it often involves a struggle with the courage to *be*, and with wanting to apologize in dialogue for their mere existence.

The need for caution

We were, however, cautious about such attempts to show that there are natural differences between the sexes, over and above the (admittedly important) biological ones. A number of reasons were given for this caution.

First, many of the so-called fundamental differences between men and women can be shown to be the result of cultural conditioning. The fact that women have given more priority to loving relationships and less to careers, for example, may result from their upbringing and from social influence. More women are now giving a higher priority to careers, which suggests that social and economic factors play a no less important role than natural ones. This is not to say that there is anything inherently wrong with being shaped by culture – we all are – but that the culture itself and the values it propagates must be tested by Christian standards.

Second, it was argued that some claims about the differences between the sexes are simply means by which men keep women in subordination. It is much easier for a man to say (and believe) that women are 'naturally' less rational and less interested in careers, than to have to admit that men have systematically oppressed women and denied them their right to education and career.

Third, it was noted that assertions about the differences between men and women are generalizations. Exceptions can always be found. This suggested that the differences between individuals were just as interesting, and perhaps more significant, than those based on gender.

Finally, it was felt by some that to set too wide a gulf between the sexes was to ignore the important fact of shared humanity. One of us writes:

> When an argument is set up dualistically, it somehow doesn't do justice to either side: we need a 'both . . . and' rather than an 'either . . . or'. But how? It is almost as if there is still incipient a half-world view which is the unspoken, unwritten feminine one, only now coming to utterance, and it can't yet be summed up in a masculine dualist discourse because it knows justice has not yet been done to it.

The lost feminine

As we argued and discussed these issues, we tried to work with the lost feminine dimension – lost during those four thousand years of our Judaeo-

Christian tradition which have been labelled the patriarchal age. The word is often used as a term of opprobrium, so as to emphasize what is seen as the domination of men over women, and point to the dire consequences in our own generation of the triumph of the supposed 'masculine mentality' in our technological, materialistic and dehumanized culture. But such language is an overstatement which leaves out of account the ways in which women's power has been exercised over the millennia, and overlooks the fact that women can be as short-sighted about consumerism and as avaricious as men. Yet it makes us conscious of the profound change which came over people's understanding of God and of themselves around 2000BC, alike in Greek culture, where male deities now dominated, and in the Jewish culture where God on high was to be worshipped as the Father and King. In the Judaeo-Christian tradition this change has been regarded as part of God's revelation of Himself. From that time, most of our religious metaphors have been masculine, and the feminine has been lost and gone underground, from whence, like all repressed matter, it keeps returning and providing a resistance movement.

If women are now to bring into the ordained ministry their embodied realities, there will be a major shift in our symbolic structure – to metaphors and symbols drawn from the womb, from the breast, from birth and nourishment; from feelings and relationships; from the menstrual and other rhythms which are constant in their inconstancy. This would be a stupendous shift, needing time to allow people to adjust their whole mind-set.

Primitive and deep responses emerge when we become involved in the debate about men, women and priesthood: women's fear of the phallic and abandoning male; men's fear of the engulfing, trapping powers of the female, which are often expressed in terms of revulsion over body, blood, milk – the terror that a pregnant woman might administer the sacrament, or even a menstruating woman. Where do these deep fears come from? Are they fears of sexuality? Or, in men, the fear of the submerging and possessing mother against whom they must fight for their independence? There is a special nervousness concentrated around the word sacrifice: women, it is said, cannot offer sacrifice (as is still the rule in, for example, Papua New Guinea). If we are thinking in terms of the bloody sacrifice of animals, then it might well be thought inappropriate for women to slit the throat of a sheep and to watch its convulsions as its lifeblood gushes out. Yet should this in fact be our dominant model for sacrifice? We should also remember the women whose whole life is an unbloody and joyful sacrifice for their husbands, children, families, neighbours and society.

As we discussed the lost feminine, we were conscious of the place of Mary in the Christian tradition. Since the Reformation the reformed Churches have underplayed the role of Mary, and lost the experience of her as our human representative in the drama of redemption. In the Anglican tradition what has been written about Mary has received very little attention. In the Orthodox and Roman Catholic Churches that experience is alive, and through Mary the attitude to the feminine is different, though equally open to criticism. Women can be touched by many of the male representations of Mary as an idealized woman because it offers us a glimpse of the tender depths of man's soul. Yet women are uneasy about this image as it does not represent for them the fullness and richness of woman's experience. It is noticeable how creative women are struggling with imagery that needs to incorporate the dark and destructive aspects in women's spiritual and psychological potency and fertility, to hold them in creative tension with other more traditionally acceptable aspects. This brings some women towards Mary with a new sense of urgency and longing for a deeper dialogue about what she can reveal to us. Mary is the mother from whose womb Jesus came, from whose breast he sucked milk, from whose teaching He learnt the Jewish faith. From a human point of view she was potentially the possessing mother from whom he must break free, but mother and Son achieved their necessary separation together. So at the end of His life she was able to stand by the cross and share in His sacrifice. In the climax of St John's Gospel Jesus gives John to Mary with the words, 'Woman, behold your son', and Mary to John with the words, 'Behold your mother' (John 19.27). One of our group writes:

> These words are the climax of St John's Gospel, the fulfilment of the New Commandment, 'Love one another' (John 13.34) and of the prayer 'that they may be one' (John 17.21). 'After this', John continues, 'Jesus knew that all things were now accomplished' (John 19.28). Now the new creation has begun, for which His life is being given on the cross. Now the two people who love Him most are being made one. Now, as He hands over His spirit to them, John will be Christ and Mary will give birth to Christ – in the to and fro of love between them John will become one with Christ as Mary enables Christ to come to birth in his soul.
>
> Does this symbolize the ultimate complementarity in the Spirit between men and women?
>
> 'Being Christ' and 'giving birth to Christ' are complementary gifts of the same Holy Spirit, but we have gone only half-way into the truth of the new creation by saying 'John will be Christ and Mary will give birth to Christ'. These are separate aspects of the whole truth, and of those separate aspects John and Mary are the guardians. But John will be Christ only as he gives birth to Christ, and Mary will give birth to Christ only through being Christ. They appear in time to have different roles as a man and a woman, as Son and Mother; but in eternal life those differences have been transformed into the Communion of the Holy Spirit.

The women of a Greek Orthodox parish in Athens were giving lunch to a group of Anglican clergy, and after lunch they talked together about the place of women in the Church. 'Do you not mind being treated as inferior?' asked one of the clergy. 'Inferior?' replied one of the women. 'But we gave birth to Christ!'

The crux

What answer can we give to the 'crucial question' with which we started? Our discussion of the complementarity of men and women began with the story of creation, and reaches its fulfilment in the story of redemption. It is significant that the word crucial means confronting the crux, or the cross; and that as we confront the cross we find the man and the woman whom Jesus loved being made one in a new relationship. They are different, and they are made one, and God's purpose in creation is accomplished in a new creation. They are held together by the energy of God's love, as in their embodied differences the spirit of the risen Christ comes alive.

Does this throw any light on 'The complementarity of men and women in ministry' and on the question 'What sort of ministry does God want?'

2
Scripture and tradition

In these discussions our own experience ran parallel to and interacted continually with the evidence of Scripture and tradition. What did our Jewish forerunners, and those fellow Christians who lived and died before us, have to say about the complementarity of men and women?

The Bible

The Bible does not have much to say directly about the differences between the sexes, and the forms of ministry appropriate to them.

The creation story, however, opens up the question of their complementarity. There are in fact two creation stories recorded in Genesis. In the first, as we have already seen, the difference between men and women within their common humanity is part of God's design, and through their partnership He reveals His own image (Genesis 1.26 – 28). In the second, man is prior to woman, but God says 'It is not good that man should be alone' (Genesis 2.18) and woman is created to help him. The man and his wife are joined together and they constitute one flesh (one human nature and personality). They are naked and unashamed.

In the story of the Fall, Adam and Eve play different roles. The blame is put on Eve, both in the Jewish story and in its interpretation in Christian writing, as in the ancient Orthodox hymn, 'O Paradise, given by God to Adam, and lost by Eve'. But if, as William Temple suggested, the Fall is in a sense a fall upwards, then Eve may appear as the more courageous one who dares to break free of a childish dependence on God, and to awaken in Adam and herself an awareness of their sexuality. They sew fig leaves together and make themselves loincloths. But as a consequence of their disobedience a childlike innocence and harmony is broken, and the domination of men over women begins.

In the Old Testament, generally speaking, there is a tension between the fact that the salvific will of God embraces men and women equally – so that they have fundamental equality – and the fact that in practice women are treated as inferior to men and discriminated against by Jewish law. But we should stress that women in ancient Jewish society have a relatively high status when compared with other contemporary societies, and that women play a significant part in the Bible story. Abraham and Sarah, Isaac and Rebecca, Jacob and Rachel, are partners together in the human story through which God speaks. Deborah is a leader in war and peace, and the poetic version of her story is probably one of the oldest passages in the Bible, giving an important clue to the position of noble women in Hebrew society in the period of the Judges. Ruth is a model of the loyal wife; and in the Song of Songs is expressed the beauty of erotic love between a man and a woman which reflects the love between God and the human soul. There is no direct teaching about the differences between the genders and their appropriate ministries in religious ritual. It was taken for granted that priests serving JHWH would be men. Only in a time of apostasy would women, together with their husbands, pour out drink offerings to the Queen of Heaven. Originally priests as a class did not exist, and any Israelite man could present offerings to God – as, for example, Abraham offering a ram in place of his son, or Gideon offering a bull. Later the privilege of offering sacrifice was confined to a priestly caste: the Levites, descendants of Aaron, first appointed in the Sinai wilderness, whose responsibilities grew rapidly and changed with the changing conditions of Israel over fourteen centuries.

In the New Testament, the ministry of Jesus is to men and women equally. Women come to Him for healing and bring their children to Him. The images in His teaching are drawn as much from a woman's world as from a man's world. He breaks taboos by entering into a profound conversation with the Samaritan woman (John 4) and ministering to women who are socially outcast and ritually unclean (Matthew 9.20). He allows a woman to anoint His feet with her hair (Luke 7.38; cf Matthew 26.7; John 12.3). His intimate friends include the sisters of Lazarus, Martha and Mary. Women stand beside His cross and are the first witnesses of His resurrection.

On the other hand, Jesus does not include women – not even His mother Mary – among the twelve apostles. To no woman does Christ say, 'He who hears you, hears me' (Luke 10.16), and to no woman does He make the promise to ratify in heaven what she has bound or loosed on earth (Matthew 16.19; 18.18). No woman, so it would seem, participated in the Last Supper – although women may well have been present at Pentecost (Acts 1.14).

Yet how conclusive is this for the ordination issue? The Twelve, on the view of many biblical scholars, are to be regarded as an eschatological sign of the new Israel which is now at hand: they represent the twelve sons and the twelve tribes of Israel, and are not appointed as leaders of a future Church. In fact, James the brother of the Lord, who is not one of the Twelve, emerges as the head of the Church at Jerusalem, rivalling Peter in importance, presiding over the Council as it makes radical decisions, and receiving the report of Paul's missionary journey (Acts 15.13; cf Galatians 1.19). None the less it remains true that in the New Testament no woman exercises a ministry of Church leadership.

The writings of Paul present us with a difficulty, in that there appear to be contradictions in his own thinking. On the one hand he declares that 'all who have been baptised in Christ have put on Christ . . . there is neither male nor female: for you are all one in Christ Jesus' (Galatians 3.27, 28). On the other hand he says that 'A man is the image and glory of God; but woman is the glory of man. For man is not from woman, but woman from man. Nor was man created for the woman, but woman for the man' (1 Corinthians 11.7 – 9). Paul seems to be echoing the two creation stories. We should be careful not to accuse such a great and inspired thinker of confusion; it may be that he reflects the mind of God, in whom opposites coincide. In any case, he concludes this second passage: 'Nevertheless, neither is man without woman, nor woman without man. For as the woman was from the man, even so also the man is through the woman; but all things are from God' (1 Corinthians 11.11 – 12).

This ambiguity in Paul's thinking is reflected in the structure of the early Church, as we catch glimpses of it in the pages of the New Testament. On the one hand, the Pauline communities seem to accept ministerial roles for women: Priscilla and Aquila, husband and wife, are *both* Paul's fellow workers (Acts 18.26; Romans 16.3; 2 Timothy 4.19). He speaks of Euodia and Syntyche, who have a disagreement, as 'these women who laboured with me in the gospel' (Philippians 4.2 – 3). Phoebe is called a deacon (*diakonos*, the Greek masculine form) although this could mean *servant* rather than deacon (Romans 16.1). Andronicus and Junias are called 'my kinsmen and fellow prisoners who are of note among the apostles' (Romans 16.7). Tryphaena and Tryphosa, and the beloved Persis, are all sent special greetings as those who have 'laboured in the Lord' (Romans 16.12). At Laodicea, Paul greets Nympha (Colossians 4.15) who, together with other women, like Phoebe at Cenchraea (Romans 16.1) and Lydia at Philippi (Acts 16.14), had allowed her home to become a domestic Church. When he stays with Philip the Evangelist he meets Philip's four daughters who are prophetesses (Acts 21.9).

This is the picture we gather from The Acts of the Apostles and from Paul's great Epistles, according to Hervé Legrand, a Roman Catholic theologian, in his essay: 'The non-ordination of women: tradition òr simply an historical fact?' (*Worship*, Vol 65, no 6, Nov 1991). He believes that in the deutero-Pauline Church, as we gather from the lesser and later Epistles, this picture has changed. Now women are excluded, as in 1 Timothy 2.11 – 15: 'A woman must listen in silence and be completely submissive. I do not permit a woman to act as teacher, or in any way to have authority over a man.' Legrand believes that the change is not derived from the example of Jesus or from the practice of the early Church; it is due to cultural pressures, for the Church is adopting the household codes which were found in Jewish Hellenism, and which prescribe the submission of the wife to the husband, children to their parents, slaves to their masters. Legrand notes that the one exception to this pattern is in 1 Corinthians, which is amongst the first group of the great Pauline Epistles. But, as we have already noticed, there appears to be some ambiguity or complementarity in Paul's own thinking and, while in 1 Corinthians 11.3 – 15 he is in fact authorizing women to pray out loud and to prophesy provided their heads are covered, in 1 Corinthians 14.34 – 5 he seems to withdraw this permission.

Legrand concludes from the biblical evidence that the non-ordination of women and their subordination to men is not a divine tradition, based on the order of creation or on the example of Jesus, but a wholly apostolic tradition (*traditio mere apostolica*); and that, while it is an undeniable historical fact that women have never been ordained to the order of priest or bishop, it could be argued that this is not necessarily divine tradition but something which emerges for a second generation. But there are of course others who still remain convinced that the action of Christ, in not choosing any women among the twelve apostles, constitutes a binding precedent.

The tradition

The living tradition of the Church is more than a set of rules, and more than historical repetition. It is also the unbroken continuity of prayer and spiritual life within the Church. As von Hügel says, 'Behind every saint stands another saint.'

The word *tradition* (in Greek *paradosis*) means literally 'handing over'. It is the handing over from one person to another, and from one generation to another, of the truth of the living God. It is a daily return to the 'steadfast mercy' of the God who said to Moses: 'I am the God of your fathers, the God of Abraham, the God of Isaac, the God of Jacob' (Exodus 3.6). It is a return to the past – but, as the Orthodox theologian Alexander Schmemann puts it, 'not to the past as past, but to that in the past which transcends the fragmentation of time into past, present and future, to that which must shape the Church's "today" as it shaped the "yesterday" and, hopefully, shall shape its "tomorrow"'.

This tradition, or handing over, is very different from the blind and inflexible traditionalism into which it can degenerate. Jesus was attacked by the traditionalists because he did not in their view keep the *paradosis* of their ancestors: His disciples ate with unwashed hands, and He himself relaxed the Sabbath rules to do works of mercy. He replied: 'You neglect the Commandment of God in order to maintain the tradition of men. . . . Thus by your own tradition, handed down among you, you make God's word null and void' (Mark 8.9, 13). He allowed women to touch him (Luke 8.43 – 8) and He Himself touched lepers (Matthew 8.3) and dead corpses (Luke 7.14).

This difference between tradition and traditionalism is poignantly illustrated at the crucifixion of Jesus. The word *paradosis* is used for the handing over of Jesus to the Jewish and the Roman authorities. This is inaccurately translated into English as 'betrayal' whereas the Greek word for betrayal is *prodosis*. The sin of Judas was not so much to betray Jesus as to treat Him as an object to be handed over. The word *paradosis* is also used of Jesus handing over Himself, at the very moment of His death: 'He said "It is accomplished." And bowing His head he handed over His spirit' (John 19.30). Here is the source of our Christian tradition: God is handing over His spirit for us, to become in us a fountain of living water. That is the truth to which we must return daily. In traditionalism, on the other hand, we are treating the Spirit of God as an object we can comprehend, codify and hand over to our descendants. Within this one word lie two terrifying possibilities of good and evil – the presence of the living God, and the blasphemy against the Holy Spirit.

As we searched within tradition for guidance about the ordination of women, we asked ourselves how conclusive was the silence of the evidence. Silence can be interpreted in two ways: does it imply a prohibition, or does it simply leave the question open? Scripture nowhere specifically advocates the ordination of women as priests, but it nowhere specifically forbids this. The matter was occasionally discussed in the early Church, but never in any depth. At their meeting with the Anglicans in Athens in 1978, the Orthodox simply appealed to the agreed fact that it has never been done. The Orthodox delegates saw this as decisive: if Christ had wished women to be priests, they said, He would have made His will clear to the apostles, and they would have obeyed Him; after two thousand years, in a matter of such importance we do not have the right to innovate. The argument from liturgical symbolism was not used. In a similar way, the 1976 Vatican decree *Inter Insigniores* confirms the existing norm: 'The Church, faithful to the example of her Lord, does not consider itself authorized to admit women to orders.' In explaining this decision, the decree declares that New Testament texts are not the whole reason. 'Exegesis of a purely historical kind is not sufficient.' Equally, symbolic arguments (such as the male priest acting *in persona Christi* during the celebration of the Eucharist) are not adduced as the main reason (we will return to this in chapter 6). As Legrand says in the article already quoted,

> The decree makes a decision on one point only. The Church does not feel authorized to ordain women to the pastoral office for the simple reason that this has never been done. She sees in this fact a norm which reflects Christ's own attitude.

Legrand asks, 'What is the doctrinal authority for such a statement?' and we still have to ask, with him, does this silence of the tradition and this historical fact, of an unbroken practice over two millennia, necessarily reflect the mind of Christ? Should we recognize in it the word of God 'which must shape the Church's "today" as it shaped the "yesterday" and, hopefully, shall shape its "tomorrow"'? Or is it 'the tradition of men which makes God's word null and void', and which frustrates the Holy Spirit, in our generation, who is seeking to 'lead us into all truth' (John 16.13)? Is it living tradition or fossilized traditionalism?

The nature of God

Behind our exploration of Scripture and tradition lay an uneasy awareness that the Bible was written by men, and the tradition formulated by men. Does this make the evidence somewhat partial? The overwhelming majority of the voices which are heard are the voices of men – judges, kings, prophets, apostles and evangelists. But they include the voice of Jesus himself. Does Jesus speak in accord with the patriarchal age in which he lives? Or is He the incarnate Word of God, who speaks the eternal truth?

This brings us face to face with the most fundamental question of all. Jesus speaks of God as Father, using a masculine epithet. *Abba*, Father, is a tender word, light-years away from the images of the male gods in the Greek pantheon, but nevertheless it is masculine. In the Bible and also in Christian tradition, most of the images of God are masculine.

The Christian confession of God as Father has never been taken to imply that God is male. This was expressed recently for Anglicans in a resolution of the Lambeth Conference of 1978:

> God is not masculine. Neither is God feminine. God is the source of masculinity and femininity, and of all those human characteristics which are variously called masculine and feminine in different cultures. God's nature is reflected in the balance and interaction between them.

But, as we have already noted, the overwhelming preponderance of the symbols of God in our tradition for the last four thousand years have been masculine. There are elements of traditional teaching which counterbalance this masculine approach: in the Old Testament the concept of Wisdom, and the imagery of God as Mother – 'as one whom his mother comforts, so will I comfort you' (Isaiah 66.13); in the Christian tradition, the place of Mary in the gospel story, the use of feminine imagery in relation to the Holy Spirit in the early Syriac tradition, and the concept of Jesus as our mother, to be found in some Western mediaeval mystics. It should also be noted that, while the metaphor of mother is used to express God's feminine aspect, God is not actually invoked as mother anywhere in Scripture or liturgy. For some of us, this distinction between metaphor and invocation seemed important.

We agreed that in the world of Reformation Christianity the virtual disappearance of Mary from Christian faith and prayer has greatly increased the imbalance between the masculine and the feminine. Her neglect by Protestants and her exaltation by Catholics have made it harder to appreciate her true significance as a real human woman whose body carried the Son of God and whose love sustained Him. The development of a sane and balanced Mariology on the part of all Christians would help to resolve our present problems.

Together with masculine symbols goes masculine language. This is a problem, for we cannot truly speak of God as He or She, splitting the genders, nor as It, for God is personal. We cannot describe God by saying 'He is' or 'She is' or 'It is'. But when Moses asks 'What is your name?' God replies 'I AM'.

This brings us to the next theme in our search.

3

The Holy Trinity

'The Catholic faith is this', declares the Athanasian Creed, 'that we worship one God in Trinity, and Trinity in unity.' Not that we comprehend, but that we worship.

The Church and its ministry, if it is to be 'the ministry God wants', must reflect this mystery of the Trinity. It must represent in time, yesterday and today and tomorrow, this eternal truth – the glory of the Father and of the Son and of the Holy Spirit, as it was in the beginning, is now, and shall be for ever.

Their glory is seen in their complementarity. The Orthodox Church, knowing that we cannot paint the likeness of God, has agreed to express the glory of the Trinity through an icon which depicts the three angels who visited Abraham (Genesis 18). They are seated round a table, motionless but in a dance of love. The lines of their bodies and the colours of their clothing flow in a communion with each other which represents the Trinity in unity. The first angel looks at the second, who looks at the third, who looks deep within. In the centre of the table is a cup.

This to-and-fro of love between Father, Son and Spirit is called in the Greek tradition the *perichoresis. Peri* means around; *chora* is a place. They are giving place to each other – or giving authority to each other. The Son says, 'I can do nothing out of myself, but only what I see the Father doing' (John 5.19). The Father reveals to the Son everything that he himself is doing and gives to the Son authority to do likewise (John 5.20 – 2). In the Holy Spirit this truth of the giving and receiving of authority, which is the very being of God, comes to us when we cry for help to guide us into all truth. 'For He [the Spirit] will not speak out of Himself, but whatever He hears He will speak.' He does not seek power for Himself, but gives authority to the Father and to the Son. 'And he will announce to you things to come' (John 16.13) – He will guide us along the way to our eternal destiny.

So the heart of the *perichoresis*, of that to and fro of love, is the giving of authority to each other and the receiving of authority from each other. Authority is not the same as power; it is the spontaneous flow of truth coming out of the creative centre of an author. The essence of the Trinity is not a power-sharing but a self-emptying through which they recognize and set free the truth in each other, so that the three become one. This self-emptying for others is the agape of God ('greater love has no one'). It is symbolized by the cup on the table in the middle between them.

28

What light does this throw on our present debate about the complementarity of men and women in the ministry of God's Church?

Persons in community

We are to worship the God who is One Being in three persons, and whose name is I AM. He is not a monistic 'I', an individual, dwelling alone ('One is one and all alone and evermore shall be so') but 'I AM' whose being consists in relations, and in the mutual indwelling of I, Thou and We. To worship such a God in Spirit and in truth we too must be not individuals but persons – persons in community with each other. So Jesus prays for us 'that they all may be one, as you, Father, are in me, and I in you, that they also may be one in us, so that the world may believe that you sent me. And the glory which you gave me I have given them, that they may be one just as we are one' (John 17.21 – 2). If the glory of the Father and of the Son and of the Holy Spirit is to be in the Church, as Jesus prayed and Paul after Him, then the Church must be a holy communion in which we recognize the authority of God in each other, and in which the heart of our communion is a self-emptying for each other.

Recognizing the authority of God in each other

When any Church community debates the ordination of women, we would expect both men and women to recognize the image of God in each other. In the Western tradition, the monarchian tendency in understanding Trinitarian doctrine has all too frequently produced an understanding of God which is cast in terms of monistic will rather than *perichoresis* and *kenosis*. It is not without significance that it is the West that has produced the remote God of Deism; the inscrutable, predestinating God of Calvinism; and forensic understandings of atonement. It is the West also which has (perhaps by displacement of such a God) produced images of Promethean man, and distorted understandings of humanity in various forms of power-dominant masculinity, with corresponding distortions in our understanding of women as subservient and passive. (We must not put too much blame on the West. Eastern Christians are not always *kenotic*, and certainly women in the Christian East have been seen as 'subservient and passive'.) A recovery of a true Trinitarianism should enable a recovery of the place of *kenosis* in any true understanding of masculinity, and of the loving affirmation which bestows self-confidence in a truly complementary understanding of the feminine.

One of us wrote:

We would expect the men to be recognizing the authority of God in the women; the women to be recognizing the authority of God in the men; and both to be speaking out of their own self-emptying. The men might be saying:

> 'Come and help us. We have been guilty of heresy. We have made an image of God as masculine. Not only that, but we have "imagined" him in the distorting mirror of our own sinful masculinity, and we have projected onto him the demonic values of our power-seeking patriarchal society. So we have lost the true vision not only of God but also of masculinity, and of ourselves as men. Come and help us, for we see God in you. We need you, whom we have so often oppressed. Be women, so that men may be men, and we may know God together.'

The women might also be saying:

> 'Come and help us. For we have lost our sense of self-worth – that too is heresy. We lack the courage to be. We have a voice that is different from yours, and a way of understanding which is less intellectual and abstract, more personal and playful; our spiritual path, though the same, is yet different; our prayer more like giving birth; our God experienced as both Father and Mother. But you seem afraid to listen to us, and to get involved in relations with us. Are you afraid of the possessive love of your mothers? Forgive us that imperfect loving! Help us to rediscover together the wholeness of God, and of ourselves made in His image. We need your human masculinity, and we recognize God's authority in you. Through our love may God give you back your true manhood and as you receive it from us, we shall rejoice to be women.'

Worshipping the Father in the Spirit

Within the worship of God who is One Being in Three Persons, we come to know that those three persons are not masculine or feminine, but the source of masculinity and femininity.

At first sight it would appear that the Father and the Son are intrinsically masculine. Deeper reflection shows us that these names cannot be literal descriptions of God, but are given to us as metaphors through which we are attracted to Him, and as titles or invocations through which we are taught to worship Him. Within our normal understanding of the term, God is not our father who sends sperm to fertilize our mother; He does not father Adam and Eve, He creates them. But God is *like* a father, in that without Him we would not exist. He is *like* a father who loves us and who lives in us. He is *like* a father who has compassion on us, and who welcomes us when we come back home; a father who trusts us to manage His property, and sends us out as His representatives to advance His work. These images kindle our worship. But God is also *like* a mother who gives us birth, who holds us and feeds us, whose self-giving love supports us throughout our lives. These images also kindle our worship.

When Jesus was speaking *about* God he used the word Father. But when He spoke directly *to* God he used the invocation Abba, the word which little children use in the security of their own homes, as they prattle away to their fathers with complete freedom about whatever concerns them. Unless we become as little children we cannot enter with Jesus into the mystery of that relation with God. 'Abba/Father' seems to affirm both the tenderness and the authority of a father and a mother, but it is significant that Jesus said '*Abba*' and not '*Imma*', the Aramaic for mother. In using the masculine form, He was remaining true to His own Jewish tradition of worship, and at the same time opening a door to a new understanding of God's fatherhood. He tells the Samaritan woman that the old ways of worship are being superseded. 'The hour is coming and now is', he says to her, 'when true worshippers will worship the Father in Spirit and in truth. For the Father is seeking such worshippers. God is Spirit, and those who worship Him must worship in Spirit and in truth' (John 4.23 – 4).

The third person of the Holy Trinity is presented to us by Scripture and tradition in both masculine and feminine terms. The Spirit is the breath of God, the living water, the divine wisdom who is creative and playful. As the giver of life, the Spirit is both our Lord and our mother. The metaphor of mother does not contradict or interfere with the metaphor of father, for in the Spirit the opposites coincide. Above all, as Jesus told His disciples, the Spirit is 'the Spirit of Truth'. The Greek word for truth is *aletheia*: a = not, and *lethe* = the river of forgetfulness: the Spirit is not letting us forget, but is calling to mind what was in the beginning, is now, and ever shall be. He is the free gift to the disciples of eternity breaking into time. Speaking out of that eternal reality He will tell them things to come, and guide them into an ever clearer consciousness of God.

We must trust, then, that if we 'worship the Father in Spirit and in truth' we shall be guided into a fuller knowledge of His fatherhood. The metaphor of father is there not to imprison us in a definition, but for the Spirit to play with, and to lead us on our way home.

Each person of the Trinity represents the wholeness of God, and together they reveal to us God's Being. This brings us to our next theme, to the second person of the Trinity, who says 'I AM the way' (John 14.6). If we are to come home, we must worship the Father not only in the Spirit but also through the Son, who became flesh and lived among us as a masculine human being. What does His incarnation reveal to us about the complementarity of men and women in the ministry of His Church?

4

The incarnation

We cannot answer the question, 'What is priesthood in the Christian Church?' without first asking: 'Who is Christ incarnate?'

The incarnate Christ Himself, in the first chapter of St John's Gospel, begins to answer both these questions. As he chooses his first disciples, he says to them: 'You will see heaven opened and the angels of God going up and coming down upon the Son of Man' (John 1.51). This is an image of who He is, and this is the nature of His priesthood.

This is who He is. He is that ladder of which Jacob dreamed, 'set up on earth and its top reached to heaven', the ladder between humankind and God, between the deviousness of Jacob and the steadfast mercy of God. 'The angels of God were going up and coming down upon it', carrying Jacob's human nature up to God, and bringing God's mercy and truth down to Jacob (Genesis 28.12 – 13). Jesus knows that He is that ladder, reaching from earth to heaven, and that in Him the Spirit of God is lifting up human nature to God and bringing down God's love to transform human nature.

This is the nature of His priesthood. In Him is the marriage of heaven and earth. He is *theanthropos*, at once human and divine, our great High Priest, who mediates between God and human beings. All our acts of mediation have their basis in His mediation.

Christology is therefore essential to our understanding of priesthood, for the priestly ministry in the Church must in some sense represent Christ: in what sense, we shall discuss later.

Masculine and feminine in Christ

We worship Christ in masculine language as the eternal Son, 'begotten of His Father before all worlds'. All our language about God, as we have already noted, is inevitably symbolical. We must never forget the mystery of God, and that theology must always be apophatic, content in the end to say what God is not rather than seeking to define what He is. When we speak of Father and Son, and when we refer to the *eternal generation* of the Son, obviously we are using language which is not to be taken literally. Yet symbolism is profoundly significant, as it points us towards the truth lying within the mystery. The fact that we are baptized in the name of the Father and the Son, not of the Mother and the Daughter, is an irreducible element in the revealed Christian faith that we cannot alter.

Yet Christ, as eternal Son of God, is described as both *Logos* (John 1.1) and *Sophia* (1 Corinthians 1.24), and these appear to be contrasting masculine and feminine principles. Logos, the Word of God, is the rational principle which gives unity and significance to all created things; it is law and order, the ruling fact of the universe. Sophia, the Wisdom of God, differs from Logos above all in that it emphasises feeling, joy, delight, playfulness; it is the bond of mutual love between God and humanity. 'I was daily his delight', says Wisdom, 'rejoicing always before him, rejoicing in his inhabited world, and my delight was with the sons of men' (Proverbs 8.30). As we have already discovered, it is difficult (if not impossible) to say definitively of any quality, 'this is masculine' or 'this is feminine'; but Logos and Sophia are two different ways of talking about Christ which correspond to our 'feeling' of what is masculine and feminine, and call out of us two different responses to God. We have no authority in Scripture or Tradition for speaking of the second person of the Trinity as God the Daughter. But we need to find a place in our vision of Christ for this feminine imagery of Sophia, and this confirms our earlier conclusion that no person of the Trinity can be described in exclusively masculine or exclusively feminine language.

The incarnate Christ is both *anthropos* and *aner*, both human and male. However, it is the first of these aspects which is emphasized in the Creed: 'and became human' – *enanthropisen*. For us humans, and for our salvation, He became human; in the Christian doctrine of salvation, the essential point is not the masculinity of Christ but His humanity. Christ heals and saves us by taking up our total humanity into Himself: 'The unassumed is unhealed', says St Gregory of Nazianzus. Obviously He is the saviour not just of males but of humankind, men and women alike. If what matters soteriologically about Christ the high priest is His humanness, why should He not be represented as much by women as by men – both in the Eucharist and in sacramental absolution? In the Eucharist we 'see heaven opened' and Christ is the ladder between earth and heaven on which the Spirit ascends and descends: he accepts the whole of human nature, and offers it up to God in thanksgiving; then He breaks it and gives it to us. If priests at the Eucharist are to represent that offering of human nature to God, should they not include both men and women and, if they are to represent that gift of God's Spirit to us, then should their priesthood not be both masculine and feminine? Similarly in the sacrament of absolution, our great High Priest carries our sins to God, and brings God's mercy to us. Might it not be more appropriate and effective if men and women were available to represent Him together in carrying the sins of the world to God, and in declaring God's forgiveness and peace to the world?

The victory of the cross

But there is nothing arbitrary or casual about God's act of salvation. If the Saviour was in fact a man and not a woman, must that not have a theological significance? We have to remember that the Lord's Prayer ends not with our need for bread or forgiveness, but with the cry of utter helplessness: 'Rescue us from evil'. The sins of the world are far more than our own personal sins. They are the sins of a whole structure of evil, centred upon a clinging onto power.

It is this structure of evil in which we are imprisoned that the Saviour defeats, and He defeats it through becoming powerless on the cross. We may ask: 'Could it have been a woman on the cross, or did it have to be a man?' The answer seems to be that it had to be a man. Both because women were not crucified by the Romans, and because the battle with 'the powers of the world' was at that moment in history a battle with a masculine power structure. Only a man, by becoming powerless, could have defeated Pontius Pilate and Caiaphas, and through them the demonic power at the heart of all human power structures. If the Saviour had been a woman, it would have been a different story: none the less horrific, but different. In our gospel story a Jewish mother stands by the cross and watches her son die; a different story would have different dynamics, and different repercussions in ourselves. Does the manhood of Jesus point to a special role for male priests? As one of the men in our group said to us:

> At the Eucharist we remember how, at a particular moment in history and through a bloody sacrifice, Jesus handed over His humanity to God in the struggle against the evil powers of a masculine world-order. It is right that men and women together, sharing in the priesthood of all believers, should live out the Eucharist of His death and resurrection; but is there a masculine role within our common humanity, that we men, acting as forgiven sinners on behalf of the whole Church, should in our central act of remembering humbly and joyfully re-present the laying down of His manhood in the victory of Love over wicked men?

The Christian tradition has not so far given much thought to the specific maleness of Christ, and here is a theme which calls for further exploration. Perhaps our own age is being called to embark on this new and exploratory task; it is unsafe to argue simply from the silence of the tradition, as it is always unsafe to argue simply from silence. There are signs that our own generation is becoming conscious of the need to rediscover the meaning of true masculinity. In a culture where fathers are generally experienced as absent fathers, and often seen as figures of fun – as trivial, irresolute and workaholic –

sons find it difficult to grow up into men; how can they become independent of their mothers, and develop into good husbands and fathers themselves, unless there is the example of a man to initiate them into manhood?

Eternity and time

We have to explore the connection between eternity and time, between God in eternity as Father and Son, and God in time as Son of the Virgin Mary. Does Christ's human maleness in some way reflect His eternal divine Sonship – I and the Father who sent me?

The crucified Christ, as He hands over His psyche to God, hands over His masculinity. The risen and ascended Christ then becomes the centre of a new creation and of a transformed humanity, where in Him there is neither male nor female.

The New Testament writers, living in the coincidence of eternity and time, speak of Christ as the Bridegroom and the Church as the Bride (Matthew 9.15; 25.1; John 3.29; Revelation 21.2, 9; 22.17). The maleness of Christ seems to possess here a symbolic significance, with theological implications. Could a woman priest represent Christ as the Bridegroom of the Church? Or does the metaphor point us beyond the Church in time to the marriage of heaven and earth, when there will be no more ecclesiastical buildings; and to that wedding feast where there will be no more sacraments; and to the New Jerusalem, where 'the Lord God Almighty and the Lamb are its temple . . . and his servants shall see his face, and his name be on their foreheads (Revelation 21.22; 22.4)?

Jesus and the tradition

We look to Jesus for guidance about priesthood in His Church, to 'Jesus Christ the same yesterday and today and for ever' (Hebrews 13.8), and we see in His incarnate life that He was true to the tradition, and at the same time He opened the door to the deeper truth hidden within it.

He said: 'Do not think I come to destroy the Law and the Prophets; I did not come to destroy but to fulfil' (Matthew 5.17).

He taught that 'not one jot or tittle shall pass from the law till all be fulfilled' (Matthew 5.18), and He revealed the grace and truth by which that fulfilment would dawn upon us.

He based His teaching on the Scriptures, but He himself taught: 'You have heard it was said to those of old . . . but I say to you . . .' (Matthew 5.21 – 2).

He was zealous for the Jewish Temple, but He declared that 'my Father's house is a house of prayer for all nations' (Mark 11.17). His mission was at first only to the Jews, but through a mother whose child was sick He came to see that God's healing was also for the gentiles.

He said: 'With desire I have desired to eat the passover' (Luke 22.15) – but within the Passover He revealed the Eucharist.

As we look to Jesus for guidance, He looks at us and says: 'I AM the way. Follow me.'

5

What does it mean to be human?

The synergy of human nature and Spirit

In the *Te Deum* we sing: 'You Christ are the King of Glory, the eternal Son of the Father. When you became human to set us free, you did not abhor the Virgin's womb.' Christ did not shrink back in horror from becoming fully and nakedly human.

In Him we see the full range of what it means to be truly human. He is hungry (Matthew 4.2) and thirsty (John 4.7); He gets tired (John 4.6) and angry (John 2.13 – 16); He is tempted by power (Matthew 4.3 – 10); He weeps with compassion (John 11.35); He loves both women and men (John 11.5); He shudders at the presence of death (John 11.33); He knows God (John 10.15). In Him the uncreated energy of God has become one with the created energy of human nature, and in that synergy (that working together) is a 'new creation'. Jesus the Son of Humankind (*anthropou*) is a prototype of the full humanity which will come to birth in those men and women to whom He has given authority to become the children of God.

What we see in Him, He sees potentially in us, and He sets us free to be fully human. 'I am come that they may have life and have it in all its fullness' (John 10.10). So He commands us: 'Receive the Spirit' (John 20.22) to be in you this synergy between God's love and your human nature, the Spirit who is the Lord and creator of life and who shows us that we are more earthly and more heavenly than we had hitherto dared to admit.

Priesthood and human nature

The Spirit will give us this fully human life not as individuals but as persons in community. It is a community, first, with the whole of nature, which releases and fosters all the immense diversity which God as creator has put into His universe – antelopes, seaweed, stars, snowflakes. Second, it is a community within the human family, which opens up the great richness and diversity between us, between different epochs of history, between different races and cultures, and – most germane to our present discussion – between men and women. Third, it is a community with God, for it sets free in us the to-and-fro between earth and heaven. So in making us fully human the Spirit invites us to be priests, for (as we have already seen) the essence of priesthood is that very to-and-fro between earth and heaven. The farmer who respects his pigs, conscious that they are more than objects out of which he can make money, is to that extent a natural priest. So too is the mother who sees that her new-born baby comes 'trailing clouds of glory from God who is our home'. So, too, is the child who wonders at the beauty and variety of the fresh young leaves opening in the spring-time.

Human beings have been created to know God and to be His priests. We long for such knowledge, but we shrink from it, and so in every culture the need has been recognized for special priestly persons to establish harmony between those they represent and the unseen powers. Such priestly persons have been the head of a family, a king, a Druid, a shaman, a witch-doctor, a soothsayer, a bard, or the oracle at Delphi, teaching in riddles but based on the profound wisdom, 'Know thyself'.

In the Old Testament, although the whole people of Israel is a kingdom of priests, the sons of Levi were appointed to teach them and bless them, and to offer sacrifices for them as gifts to God by which they might enter into communion with Him. In the New Testament such an order of priests is at first never mentioned. Jesus Himself has become the ladder between heaven and earth, and those who share His resurrection are priests of God and of Christ in the new creation. So there are three levels to be distinguished: there is a priesthood first of *one*, then of *all*, then of *some*. One and one only is priest: Christ the unique high priest, the one mediator (1 Timothy 2.5). All are priests: by virtue of their creation in the divine image, all humans can exercise a cosmic priesthood, offering the world back to its Maker in thanksgiving; and it is this universal priesthood according to the divine image that is renewed through Baptism, so that in Christ the entire people of God constitutes 'a royal priesthood, a holy nation' (1 Peter 2.9). At the same time some are priests – those set apart for the ordained ministry through the laying-on of hands. Yet the universal priesthood has priority over any ministerial priesthood; the whole Church expresses it, and it is reaffirmed in each one of us – men and women alike – through the sacrament at Baptism, which restores in us the image of God, our full humanity, and so our natural priesthood.

To become fully human and priests of God we must become persons in community, for the Spirit who gives us communion with each other is the Lord and creator of life; and when we speak of life we speak of both unity and diversity – of love and understanding, but also of multiplicity, spontaneity, the unexpected and the idiosyncratic. Within the all-embracing community of nature, the human family and God, the community which the Spirit brings is to be lived in freedom and diversity, as each man and woman is set free to become his or her unique self.

Priesthood and sexuality

Our sexuality is an essential part of the human nature which priests must offer
to God, as we have already discussed in Part Two, chapter 1. The more we
recognize in men and women our gender differences, the more we are aware
of our common humanity and of our need for each other. All things go by
pairs, the one correcting and completing the other; this is seen in the
relationships of husband and wife, and in Church history by the well-known
friendships between celibates such as Benedict and Scholastica, John
Chrysostom and Olympias, Francis and Clare, Teresa of Avila and John of the
Cross, Hans Urs von Balthasar and Adrienne von Speyr. Within the body of
the Church, as within the body of humanity at large, we have to recognize our
diversity of gifts and callings; that the married need the single, and the single
need the married; that those drawn towards their own sex and those drawn
towards the other sex need each others' company in relationships of mutual
trust, respect and affection. As we find out how much we need each other, we
find also that we have unsuspected gifts for each other.

But our sexuality is far more than a gender difference, and more than
friendship. It is erotic love springing out of the deep centre of our being.
Thanksgiving for this erotic love, amongst all the other gifts of creation, may
be rightly seen as an integral part of men and women, an aspect of the self-
offering of the universal priesthood. As they lift human nature from earth to
heaven, they have to accept as a gift from God the energy of eros, and to
thank Him for all the sparkle and the joy which it adds to human life in our
relationships with each other; in our home-making and the procreation of
children; in our literature and art, our dancing and our laughter and our
celebrations. But at the same time, being human themselves, the priests will
know that erotic love which is so creative can also be destructive, and that,
while it leads us into joy, it can also lead us into tragedy. So as priests of Christ
they will offer the energy of our human love to be transformed by the energy
of God's divine love; our eros to be transformed in a holy synergy with His
eros, so that it may flow out of us and into the world for healing and for peace
and justice.

To do this is part of the priesthood of all believers, and in so doing they are
repeating the pattern of the Eucharist, in which Jesus receives, gives thanks,
breaks and gives. He does this with His own body and blood and, when He
says 'do this in remembrance of me', He is commanding us not just to celebrate
the Eucharist liturgically but to do it, to live it, to be it.

Our acceptance of and thanksgiving for our sexuality has not, however,
been characteristic of the ministerial priesthood over the centuries. The voices
which come to us from our tradition have rather expressed a fear of sexuality,

in both the senses of the word we have outlined above: a fear of the gender differences, so that women have been seen as inferior and sometimes as a threat to men, and their natural bodily functions and menstruation as making them unclean and unfit to approach the sanctuary of God; a fear also of erotic love so that married priests who had sexual intercourse with their wives on the previous evening were unfitted to preside at the Eucharist the next morning. To which the ascetics down the years might reply that in our human condition the power of erotic love is rightly to be feared – for when it is harnessed to our ego-centricity it can lead us irresistibly to destroy each other, to forget God and thus to fall short of that synergy of human and divine eros which is our own true destiny. Likewise, the priests down the ages who have followed the way of celibate chastity might testify that they have offered eros to God in obedience to that vision of total love which Jesus set before us when He said 'greater love [*agape*] has no one than this, that he lay down his psyche [his self, his life] for his friends' (John 15.13).

Celibacy

Jesus Himself was not married. At the heart of His own life was the responsive love expressing his self-offering to the Father and for the world. That love was shown in His compassion for the poor, the outcast and the wounded in spirit: in His gathering round Him the close company of the Twelve, the wider community of His disciples and of the women who journeyed with Him. That love is embodied in His ministry and brought to its total sacrificial offering in the *kenosis* (outpouring and self-emptying) of His death which reveals the *plerosis* (fullness) of that love.

His life and death celebrated in the eucharist draw all Christians into the movement of His self-offering. For some there is a calling to express that self-offering, which is always a way of love, by a life of celibacy. According to Matthew 19.11 – 12, not only Jesus' example but also His teaching commends this way as one to be followed by those called to it 'for the sake of the kingdom of heaven'. But there are also those whose singleness is by nature ('there are eunuchs born that way from their mother's womb') and those on whom it is imposed ('there are eunuchs made so by men'). Celibacy in the Christian understanding is consecrated singleness. The Syriac term *Yiḥîdāyâ*, which it is suggested lies behind the Greek *monachos* (solitary), is linked with Christ who is 'God the *Yiḥîdāyâ* in the bosom of the Father' (John 1.18). As applied to men and women it means 'single in body, single in mind and heart, and single in soul as being totally consecrated and united to the Single One, the Single Son of God the Father'. It is far removed from the crusty bachelor and the arid spinster ironically caricatured by Newman in his *Historical Sketches*:

Bachelors are just the most selfish, unaccommodating, particular and arbitrary persons in the community; while ancient spinsters are the most disagreeable, cross, gossiping and miserable of their sex. Dreariness unmitigated, a shivering and hungry spirit, a soul preying on itself, a heart without an object, affections unemployed, life wasted, self-indulgence in prosperous circumstances, envy and malice in straitened; deadness of feeling in the male specimen, impotence of feeling in the female, concentrated selfishness in both.

(quoted by F Corrigan, *Benedictine Tapestry*, 1991, p 34, cf. p 7)

It was only in the early Middle Ages in the Latin West that celibacy came to be self-evidently required of all clergy. The tradition of celibate ascetics and teachers is much older, going back to men like Clement of Alexandria in the late second century, and probably earlier. The growth of monastic life for both men and women raised the profile of celibacy, exciting admiration and emulation by others, including lay people.

At its best celibacy has been valued as an 'eschatalogical sign' and celibate witness to a willingness to give of one's life to God alone has been a precious gift to the Church. Over the centuries and into modern times, countless men and women have devoted themselves to God in this way, both in active mission and monastic seclusion. The whole Church would be the poorer were this witness to fail.

In the East the pattern was established for the parochial clergy to be married before ordination. All others were to consecrate their singleness as monks, and it was and is from the monastic communities that bishops are appointed. (Part of the impetus in the current monastic renaissance in the Coptic Church in Egypt lies in the desire of the laity to have close relations with monastic communities up and down the Nile Valley so that they may discern those with the appropriate spiritual gifts for the episcopate.)

In the West the history of celibacy amongst the non-monastic clergy is a complex and uneven one. Not all areas accepted the idea of compulsory clerical celibacy at the same time, and even today celibacy for the clergy of the Roman rite is seen as a matter of discipline rather than doctrine. There are dangers inherent in a *compulsory* clerical celibacy. There have been those looking for a life without responsibility, or for whom a permanent relationship may seem threatening. The celibate and the single need to grow and mature just as do the married. Part of that growth may be the coming together of those characteristics labelled as 'masculine' and 'feminine' within the single person. One of our number went so far as to comment that they had been present at the death-beds of a number of monks and nuns, whose faces at that moment seemed to embody both 'masculine' and 'feminine' characteristics.

Whereas for the married the way to the One is through the sacrament of the one, for the celibate the way to the One seems to be through the many. The fruitfulness of many celibate lives is disclosed in the richness of the many spiritual sons and daughters which celibacy enables. Both marriage and celibacy are vocations that are demanding as well as enriching. In Anglicanism and in the Churches of the Reformation, which repudiated the compulsory celibate clerical tradition of the mediaeval Western Church, celibacy has not always been well understood or recognized. Where it has been, the supporting structures have not always been present. Single Christians among the laity may be marginalized by an otherwise praiseworthy concern for and emphasis on the family.

Celibacy is a charism bestowed by God and not something that one can produced in oneself. To affirm that raises special questions for those attracted to their own sex who have no vocation to marriage and equally are not able to interpret their condition as an unequivocal call to celibacy. The question of what should be for them the appropriate pattern of loving, and of their way to holiness, is one of the perplexing questions facing contemporary Churches. The Roman Catholic Church, with its discipline of compulsory celibacy, may need to examine the necessary link between celibacy and priesthood, and to give consideration to the possibility of ordaining married men while valuing and supporting the unstinting service of those who have been granted the charism of celibacy. The Anglican communion, and many other Churches, may need to find in themselves the capacity to honour and affirm the ministry of those to whom God has given this specific and highly personal gift – not primarily for fulfilling personal needs but as setting them free for the service of God's Church as a sign in a world that often seeks easy and immediate gratification.

6

Ministerial priesthood

The heart and meaning of priesthood remain the same, yesterday and today and for ever. But the practice varies in our different Churches.

The emphasis is different

We might abbreviate a long discussion and point to different emphases in the practice of priesthood within our Churches: the priest empowering the community which is the body of Christ; the priest focusing God's wholeness – the marriage of the sacred and the secular; the priest ordained primarily to celebrate the Eucharist, and to bear witness to the resurrection. These different emphases are not of course mutually exclusive. Our priests, in each of these three emphases, are representing the work of the Holy Spirit within the Church.

These words, 'the Holy Spirit within the Church', can numb our senses as a mere phrase of intellectual dogma; or they can awaken us to the Holy Spirit whom we worship and glorify, to our Lord the Spirit who is the giver of life in all its amazing diversity and unity. As St Paul exclaims: 'There are diversities of gifts but the same Spirit – differences of administration but the same Lord – diversities of activities but the same God who works all in all!' (1 Corinthians 12.4 – 6). He is describing the new-born Church as a body with many different limbs and organs. There are many forms of ministry through which the Spirit works – apostles, prophets, evangelists, pastors, teachers, miracles, gifts of healing, helps, administrations, varieties of tongues. Together they will be one synergy, one communion of love, revealing on earth and in time the eternal glory of God. Diversity in unity is not to be deplored as some sort of human failure; it is the reflection of God's glory. Human sin would be 'to fall short of the glory of God' (Romans 3.23) and to concentrate the ministry in one individual.

The leadership style is different

In all our Churches the priest is a leader. He leads the worship, and is in some sense the pastor, the counsellor, the social worker, the decision-maker. But the style and perceptions of leadership vary. In the Roman Catholic Church the priest is often thought of as the teacher of the faith, teaching under the authority of the Pope; he has often been expected by his flock to exercise an almost autocratic power, with the result that instead of empowering the community he may retreat behind his priestly role and 'do it all himself'. Part of the Anglican style of leadership – at least in England – is for the priest to be a focal point for the community; he is seen as a symbol of the presence of God, and so may exercise his most powerful ministry just by being there; he is the 'parson'– sometimes the 'person' or the all-round human being, sometimes a figure of fun, not necessarily having many specific professional skills, but holding the Church together. Under both these Western styles of leadership the laity have come to feel that the Church belongs to the clergy. By contrast, in the Eastern Orthodox Church the priest is felt to be 'one of us'; his style and life has not been very different from that of his people; he may not be well educated and he will not necessarily preach, but he will lead us in liturgical worship, and the Church belongs to *us*, not to him.

These different styles have arisen partly from or theology, but partly from our culture and history. For the last four hundred years the Roman Catholic Church has fought to preserve its tradition and its unity against the Reformation and against the threat of secularism and communism. Within the Anglican Communion the Church of England – as the established Church of a great world power – has been required to discern the presence and the judgement of God within the rise and fall of an empire, and as such has developed an over-clericalized ministry. In the Orthodox world the Church in Greece has struggled to preserve Christianity under the Turkish occupation, and to keep alive the soul of a nation. The ministers of the three Churches reflect these historical situations, and it is remarkable that the Church which has been powerless and has suffered most has developed the most healthy relationship between clergy and laity. Now that the Greek clergy are better educated, their Church is in danger of becoming more clericalized.

The pattern of marriage and celibacy is different

In the Roman Catholic Church all priests and bishops are celibate, and very many are members of religious orders; in the Anglican Communion they are generally married, though the choice of a celibate vocation is respected. In the Orthodox Church the vast majority of the parish clergy are married, but they are required to marry before ordination; those who remain celibate usually take monastic vows – although they do not necessarily live in a monastery – and it is only monks who are eligible to become bishops. While the vocation of the married priest – and the vocation of the priest's wife – are respected, priority is given to the monastic clergy: it is the monk rather than the priest who is seen as the 'holy man'. This relieves the priest of what in the West can be a burden of unrealistic idealism; it also emphasizes that the laity can follow the inner mystical life, for most monks are in fact not ordained as priests.

This brief survey of the different practices within the three Churches shows us that priesthood is not monochrome, but that its eternal essence is shot through with variety in time. This unity in diversity marks the priesthood with the character of the Holy Spirit.

Whom does the priest represent?

Priesthood has a representative character, and this representation can in principle work in two directions: the priest may represent the people to God, or he may represent God to the people. In the central consecratory prayer of the Eucharist, in which of these two ways does the priest act as representative?

In the Roman Catholic and Anglican Churches of the West it has often been understood that, at the sacred moment when the priest says 'Take, eat; this is my body . . .', he is *alter Christus*. As he stands there, saying the words of Jesus and performing the actions of Jesus, he is the icon of Christ: through his body and mind and spirit, the body and mind and spirit of Jesus is present. For many it is inappropriate that the body of a woman should represent the body of Christ, and this objection should be respected.

In the Orthodox Church, however, the eucharistic consecration is understood differently. After recalling Christ's action at the Last Supper, and his words, 'Take, eat . . . Drink of it, all of you . . .', the priest then goes on to say a prayer known in Greek as the *epiclesis*, meaning in English 'the Invocation'. He prays to the Father to send down His Holy Spirit upon the bread and wine, so that they may become the Body and Blood of Christ. The priest, as he invokes the Paraclete, speaks in the plural: 'We pray and beseech and implore: Send down Your Holy Spirit . . . .' Thus, at the decisive moment in the prayer of the *anaphora* ('offering'), the priest does not take the place of Jesus, but stands in solidarity with the people. He is not representing Christ to the congregation, but the congregation to Christ.

Some scholars in the Roman Catholic Church have recently confirmed this interpretation, pointing out that the celebrant is *in persona ecclesiae* prior to being *in persona Christi*. Bernard Cook, in *Ministry of Word and Sacraments* (Philadelphia: Fortress, 1976), writes:

> The liturgical celebrant does not offer the sacrifice himself (except insofar as he shares in the community's act of sacrifice), but it is he who makes possible the reciprocal self-giving of Christ and the community, ie: their

unified sacrifice. The celebrant does lead the eucharistic assembly as it gives voice to its sacrificial decision, but it is the entire community that corporately professes this decision, and thereby offers sacrifice.

A focus of the Spirit

We might say, then, that the priest becomes the focus of Christ's Spirit in the Church. The Latin word *focus* means originally a hearth or home where people meet, and in the language of today it has come to mean a point where rays converge, an adjustment of the eye so that an image becomes clear, a centre of energy. Thus the priest is not called to be himself 'Father' but to be a symbol that this fellowship of Christians is 'my Father's house'. Not to be in himself *alter Christus* but to draw together God's people in all their diversity so that they become a prism through which the light of Christ shines. Not in himself to impersonate the Spirit, but to let the Spirit 'call to mind the truth' of the priesthood of all believers. Not to be the busy minister who does it all himself, but the wounded healer whose authority sets free the energy in others – the synergy of their human nature and God's love.

This change of heart and mind and will, this daily *metanoia*, this understanding that he is a focus of the Spirit of Christ dancing in the whole body of the Church, breaks in the priest the idealistic image of himself – and liberates the laity from the temptation to make him a substitute for God. Now they can begin to understand that to represent Christ as a priest is not to become in some mystical fashion a latter-day clone of Jesus of Nazareth. They themselves are being called into the priesthood of all believers to represent the crucified and risen Christ who is present now through the Spirit in the Church. From the parable of the sheep and the goats (Matthew 25.31 – 4), they can learn that those who represent Christ are the ones in need – those who are hungry and naked, sick or in prison – and that to represent Christ they have not only to embrace the lost ones but to *be* the lost ones. Then, with Christ, they can be that two-way ladder set up between earth and heaven; they can both represent humanity to God as they cry out for His mercy and give thanks for His grace; but also God to humanity as He comes to the poor in spirit in His compassion, in the sign of His brokenness, and as the one who serves.

The ordination of women

Men and women together exercise the natural priesthood, and the priesthood of all believers. We must now ask: 'Does God want them to exercise together the ministerial priesthood?' Woven into the theological debate are the issues of human sexuality and of power, and their relation to the Spirit.

Human Sexuality

Is it appropriate that men and women together should be the focus of Christ's Spirit in the Church?

Rational debate does not touch the deep-seated fears that are engendered in many people by the idea of the woman priest. Some of these fears are about responsibility for interpreting the tradition of the Church; others are about authority, and an adequate understanding of who can bring about change. But the deepest and most primal fears, which often sound strange to modern consciousness, seem to be about eros – about our attraction towards and our longing for unity with the other, about how men and women understand each other in their likenesses and in that mysterious otherness which each sex represents for the other.

The energies of eros are enormously creative and destructive. How are they related to agape? We were unanimous in rejecting the notion that eros and agape are opposed to each other. All human eros is, in the eucharistic life of the Church, drawn towards its centre and its meaning, its origin and its end, in the immense, holy, perichoretic energies of the Trinitarian life of God, expressed in the incarnation of the God-Man, Christ. Faced with Divine Love in its most profound interpenetrative act, how can we not tremble in primal awe as we are confronted by human eros in a state of ultimacy so profound that it eludes interpretation? Does not this wholeness of Divine Love demand, in response, a wholeness of eros and agape in ourselves, a self-abandon in which we become sexual men and women indwelt by the Spirit of God?

But good and evil are mysteriously linked, and the possibility of the best opens us to the possibility of the worst. The energies of the transcendent love, drawing us into unity within the Eucharistic Community, are so powerful that we find it difficult to recognize that they are married to the energies which drive us apart. For love is married to power. As we seek to understand the deep meaning of changes in the representative priesthood, we are beset with fears about power and its exercise in domination, overthrow, possessiveness. Again, love is married to truth and we are beset with fears about truth. The ultimate truths about our engendered humanity are at stake. Interpretive gulfs keep opening between us and threatening the temporal unity of the Church. Both these kinds of fear are difficult to enunciate; they sometimes surface in curious half-spoken metaphors that can cause great affront to our rational minds, such fears about the felt 'uncleannesses' and 'impurities' of our 'differences'. But such fears, in both men and women, reflect something of the energic depths of love, and have to be part of our understanding.

God is calling us to wholeness in holiness, in the life of the Holy Spirit in the Church. Our holiness must bring with it an understanding of eros, in its sexual as in all other forms, as we experience it in our broken and fallen state. We must recognize what a profound change in our attitude to both sexuality and spirituality would be demanded by the ordination of women to the priesthood. We must remember again the warning in the Epistle to the Hebrews that 'priesthood being changed, of necessity there is a change in the law' (Hebrews 7.12).

Yet these words contain both a warning and a promise. It is sometimes assumed that there would be little change in the priesthood, since women priests would hide their femininity; they would dress like men and behave like men. But God does not declare Himself through androgyny. It is in the complementarity of men and women that His image and His glory is revealed, and if God wants women priests then it must be His will that the masculine mode of priesthood should be changed, so that 'the priesthood being changed', the whole Church may be transformed 'into His image, from glory to glory' (2 Corinthians 3.18).

Power

Is it appropriate that both men and women should preside at the Eucharist?

The word *preside* generally connotes power and precedence. It is interesting to note that the word used for celebrating in the Orthodox tradition is '*to serve*'. At the Last Supper there was a power struggle amongst the disciples, in the presence of Jesus Himself, as to which of them should be considered the greatest, and our own debate about men and women presiding at the Eucharist often looks like a continuation of that power struggle with each side claiming the support of Almighty God. But a priest who presides (or serves) at the Eucharist has to remember the crucifixion and to announce the resurrection of Jesus, our great High Priest, who is the ladder not only between earth and heaven, but between hell and heaven. The priest calls to mind His descent into hell and His breaking the power of evil, and celebrates His ascension into heaven and the sending to us of the Holy Spirit. It does not seem appropriate that either men or women should claim the right to preside over such mysteries; they can only pray to have 'the same mind which was in Christ Jesus' who emptied himself and became powerless, 'wherefore God exalted Him' (Philippians 2.5 – 9). The only proper priests (men or women) to preside at the Eucharist are those who remember that they too are powerless, empty and vulnerable, and that the authority they have received is a free gift of Grace.

What does God want?

So we are forced back to the question in the introduction to this report: 'What sort of a ministry does God want?' Does God want women priests?

On the one hand, many believe that the Spirit has been guiding the Church over the centuries to reflect God's will in the traditional structure of its leadership, and to preserve in its communion the God-given differences and interplay between the sexes. Therefore, faced with the question of the ordination of women as priests, the official reply of the Roman Catholic Church is that we should not do it because it has never been done: 'The Church, faithful to the example of her Lord, does not consider itself authorized to admit women to orders' (*Inter Insigniores*, Vatican 1976). As the Orthodox delegates stated at the Anglican – Orthodox meeting in Athens in 1978, 'From the time of Christ and the apostles, the Church has ordained only men to the priesthood . . . . In this constant and unvarying practice we see revealed the will of God and the testimony of the Holy Spirit, and we know that the Holy Spirit does not contradict Himself.'

Some Anglicans agree. Many Roman Catholics disagree. A small but increasing number of Orthodox are beginning to ask the question, and to throw new light on the debate for the Churches in the West. Indeed, in all our various Communions there are many who believe that the Spirit is now guiding the Church to see more deeply into the truth of its own tradition, and into the meaning of its priesthood. They are convinced that 'priesthood being changed, there is of necessity a change in the law', and that a deeper understanding of priesthood will lead us into a deeper knowledge of 'the law of the Spirit of life in Christ Jesus' (Romans 8.2).

The question of authority

It is a matter of historical fact that the ministerial priesthood and episcopate have been confined to men, though the significance of this continuous tradition may be viewed in different ways, as our discussions have made clear. To depart from this continuous tradition is to make a significant change – though what that significance may be is again a matter on which opinions differ.

To make a change of this kind is not something to be done arbitrarily; there must be authority to do it, and one of the major questions for Christians is who has authority to act, and on what grounds. In a divided Church these are difficult questions to answer. For Roman Catholics such a decision would be taken by the *magisterium*, but the Pope has declared that he does not believe that he has the authority to so act because there is no basis in Scripture or in the continuous tradition of the Church. For the Orthodox Churches such a decision would need to be taken by a General Council – but Orthodoxy would likewise regard itself as bound by Scripture and tradition. Anglicans have claimed that they have no other ministry than that of the universal Church in the historic succession – a ministry therefore which is shared with Orthodox and Roman Catholics.

Those Anglican provinces which have ordained women to the priesthood and episcopate have argued that they are not changing the theological understanding of the ministry, but that the change they have made is a legitimate development, and that such a change falls within the range of issues on which it is permissible for Anglicans to make an independent decision – as, for instance, a change in the creeds would not. Other Anglicans believe that what is claimed as a common ministry cannot be altered unilaterally. While they would accept that there is legitimate theological discussion about such a change, and powerful arguments in its favour, they are not yet convinced that the arguments are conclusive; and would further argue that, where there is a disputed question in a matter touching the sacraments, even were it to be conceded that a Church might act unilaterally, it would be wrong to do so if the consequence of such an action was to introduce doubt into a previously accepted ministry.

The sharp question is: Where the authority of Scripture and tradition is largely expressed tacitly, in that the practice of the Church has been invariable, *who* is to interpret the significance of that practice; and *how* are the decisions to be made about whether this is or is not a legitimate development? There is a further question about discerning the right time-scale for such a development, if such a development be legitimate.

Conclusions

In the course of our meetings we have found ourselves coming to certain conclusions which we should like to share with fellow Christians, of whatever tradition, who are concerned about this issue.

1   We have found that the question of the ordination of women to the priesthood and episcopate is part of a larger complex of questions involving the way in which women and men relate to one another and to God within the family of the Church.

2   In the three years in which we have been meeting we have often felt that we were only beginning to touch some of the most important issues which have emerged. The variety of ways which we have followed – imaginative and symbolical as well as intellectual and discursive – has proved unexpectedly rewarding. Though we have disagreed at times, we have not found ourselves becoming acrimonious; rather, we have found a constantly renewed fascination and delight in our shared consideration of the complementarity of men and women in the Church and in all creation.

3   Our discussions have, however, been inconclusive insofar as we have not agreed on a definitive solution to the problems which have arisen. Indeed, we have come to the perhaps paradoxical conclusion that the desire for a quick and final solution to this question can be both dangerous and misleading. We believe that the Christian world is involved in a process which will take some time to work itself out.

As regards the decision which must be taken shortly by the General Synod of the Church of England, we hope that if the proposed legislation is accepted discussion of these issues will continue, and if the legislation is not accepted the discussion of these issues will likewise continue.

4   The desire for a quick solution can be expressed in the following ways:

If only those innovators who have no real concern for or understanding of the nature of the faith and tradition of the Church would go away, this question could be easily resolved.

If only those traditionalists who have no real concern for or understanding of the times in which we live and what God is saying to us through them would go away, this question could be easily resolved.

5 But neither party to this discussion is going to go away. There are serious and respectable arguments on both sides, arguments which are held with deep and carefully considered conviction. To fail to recognize this is to fail to recognize the good faith, the intelligence and the love of fellow human beings, fellow members of the body of Christ.

We ourselves in the course of these discussions have gradually come to recognize that we do not so much want to win an argument as to listen and understand, and to recognize God's authority in each other.

6 The fact that we have been unable to arrive at a resolution to this issue, while painful, does not lead us to despair, for we have found that our discussions have clarified many apparent points of division and have been fruitful in many ways, and we believe that discussions of this kind need to be carried on much more widely.

7 On the contrary, we have been led to hope and to believe that in this, as in many other controversies in Christian history, God Himself is guiding His Church and leading us towards solutions which none of us is able fully to envisage at the present.

8 The idea of complementarity has become very important for us, not only with reference to the relationships between men and women, but also with reference to the differing ways of approach which are necessary for any at all adequate appreciation of the truth. The light which comes from the mystery of the Holy Trinity, in which total unity and complete diversity are reconciled and at one, is of endless significance for a renewed understanding and living of the mystery of unity and diversity within the family of the Church. Is it possible to envisage a form of ministry which, while giving full scope to the gifts of women, would yet retain a sense of the way in which the gifts of women and of men fulfil each other?

9 The fact that all the Churches are together facing these questions is to us a great sign of hope. The fact, for instance, that the official conversations between Anglicans and Orthodox, between Anglicans and Roman Catholics, have not been broken off on account of this question is a very positive one. The Churches need to remain in contact with one another and to listen to one another, if they are to be able together to hear what God is saying in this situation.

We ourselves as a group, predominantly Orthodox, Roman Catholic and Anglican, have found as we listened to one another and sought to understand one another that our unity was strengthened and deepened. We believe that this experience is not irrelevant to our Churches, and we hope that others of our fellow Church men and women may wish to become involved in a similar process.

10 Is it perhaps providential that there are divisions in the Church, so that one group may move forward while the others watch? Will the rest of Christendom learn from the Anglicans' mistakes? Will Anglicans make the wrong move in the right direction? More fundamentally, is it possible, at the present time, that some groups of Christians may be called to act on behalf of others? Are there complementary roles given to our Churches in their present state of partial and imperfect communion? Can we support and help one another even when we do not wholly agree with one another? But such things have to be born and to grow out of a common mind between the Churches, and cannot be achieved by unilateral action.

11 The process in which all the Churches together are involved is, we believe, one of discovering what is the will of God for the complementarity of men and women in the ministry of the Church. It may perhaps be a long time before the Churches can come to a common mind on the issue. The gift of unanimity may come randomly and unexpectedly. We observe that different Churches have different perceptions of this. A move which to some in the West seems slow and hesitant, to others in the East seems swift and unrehearsed. But we are confident that the willingness to search together for a common mind is something which God will bless and indeed already blesses.

12 For Christians who long to be at one in Christ, to fail to be united on an issue of this importance is both painful and humbling. No one should underestimate the pain which the controversy causes. But we believe that the pain and the humbling may themselves become a way towards growth. It is through our blindness and weakness that God's grace—which always heals what is wounded and makes up what is lacking—can be at work bringing healing, light and new life to humankind and to all creation.

An Epilogue

One of us wrote:

I am just back from a holiday by the sea. We were staying in the cottage on the beach, and every day we watched the tide coming in and going out. Sometimes the bay was full of sea – it was all waves; at another time it was full of sand – it was all particles. It reminded me of what the quantum scientists tell us, that the very stuff of the universe has to be seen in two ways, as waves and as particles. It is in fact both, but you cannot look at both at the same time.

One evening, at twilight, I saw a man and a woman walking up and down across the beach, at the edge of the tide. Were they in love? Or were they quarrelling? Perhaps both.

But it struck me that the complementarity of the sea and the dry land is in some mysterious way like the complementarity of the woman and the man. The sea gave birth to life, and its tides move with the moon in a twenty-eight day rhythm. Then life crawled out of the sea and onto the dry land, where it developed in the sunlight and became self-conscious, and built cities and made wars. But it would be wrong to polarize, for 'mother earth' also gives birth to life, and in the sea life also develops into self-consciousness – for example in the peaceable dolphins.

God knew that life, which is a reflection of His own nature, needed the complementarity of sea and dry land. Similarly He knew that human life, if it was to develop in all its fullness, in all its tragedy and glory, needed the complementarity of a male principle and a female principle to safeguard certain truths within His own nature, and in the interaction between them to reveal His glory.

So as I saw this man and this woman walking at twilight along the edge of the tide, I thought of the creation story and how God divided the light and the darkness (Genesis 1.4), the dry land and the sea (Genesis 1.10) and the male from the female (Genesis 1.26). Life needed such complementarities. But as He divided He did not split and polarize into opposites. Through the ebb and flow of the tides, through the sea and the land together, He created a habitat for life as it emerges from the water; and so that this developing life might not be overwhelmed, He created the rocks, and said to the sea 'hitherto shalt though come but no further, and here shall thy proud waves be stayed' (Job 38.11).

It would be absurd, and indeed diabolical, to split and polarize, and to say that women are waves and men are rocks. It may be true that women often need men to say to them 'hitherto shalt thou come but no further'; but one has immediately to recognize that men often need women to say the same to them. The complementarity of men and women touches not only our sense of wonder, that through our diversity and unity God has chosen to reveal His glory; it touches also our sense of humour, of compassion and of forgiveness, as it shows us in the 'opposite' sex what we have then to recognize in ourselves.

Two quotations

Our report ends where it began, with the two mysteries. We all agreed that God created the complementarity of men and women, and that He reveals His image through it. Like the author of the Book of Proverbs, we found it both wonderful and humorous, and too complex for us to understand.

> Three things there are which are too wonderful for me,
> and a fourth which I do not understand:
> the way of a vulture in the sky,
> the way of a serpent on the rock,
> the way of a ship out to sea,
> and the way of a man with a maid. (Proverbs 30.18 – 19)

God alone can reconcile opposites, but our discussions have given us hope that, if we meet each other and talk together, and enjoy each other, He will open our eyes to see His truth in each other, and to recognize together what sort of ministry He wants.

Above all, if we pray together:

> Come, Holy Spirit of Christ in the Church,
> and dwell in our inner being,
> 'that we may be strong to grasp
> with all God's people,
> what is the breadth and length and height and depth
> of the love of Christ
> and to know it though it is beyond knowledge.
> Now to him who is able to do immeasurably more
> than all we can ask or conceive,
> by the power which is at work among us,
> to him be glory in the Church and in Christ Jesus,
> from generation to generation evermore.   Amen'.
> (Ephesians 3.18 — 21)